TESSAHOC
Arthur

Donna Fritz

authorHOUSE®

AuthorHouse™
1663 Liberty Drive
Bloomington, IN 47403
www.authorhouse.com
Phone: 1 (800) 839-8640

Published by AuthorHouse 01/13/2018

ISBN: 978-1-5462-2391-7 (sc)
ISBN: 978-1-5462-2390-0 (e)

Print information available on the last page.

"I have tried to recreate events, locales and conversations from my memories
of them. In order to maintain their anonymity in some instances I have
changed the names of individuals and places; I may have changed some
identifying characteristics and details such as physical properties, occupations,
and/or places. All images are the author's own photographs or drawings."

This book is printed on acid-free paper.

Because of the dynamic nature of the Internet, any web addresses or
links contained in this book may have changed since publication and
may no longer be valid. The views expressed in this work are solely those
of the author and do not necessarily reflect the views of the publisher,
and the publisher hereby disclaims any responsibility for them.

for
Tessahoc Arthur
My Valentine CGC

in loving memory of

Paul Girard
for driving me the long distance to go get
my new puppy, and making it fun

with special thanks to

Emerson, for being there

Lucille,
for loving Arthur and ignoring the mess he made,
helping us train (even tracking out in the snow!)
and feeding him roast beef off your plate (yes, I noticed)

Cindi,
for being a marvellous friend,
and volunteering your father as a
long-distance chauffeur

Rhonda and Tigerlily,
for the marsupial, nocturnal encouragement,
friendship beyond words, and letting me use you

Dr. Martin and Dr. Shing, and all the staff
at the Cortland Veterinary Hospital

Dr. Spindel and the staff at Animal
Ark Veterinary Service

and all of Arthur's fans,
for following his exploits, and treating him like
a celebrity when they saw him in the street.
He loved it.

Foreword

About two years after Hobbes' death, Pam called, out of the blue, to tell me that she had a dog for me, a nephew of Hobby. She said she had saved me "the marshmallow of the litter" -- this in a breed known for a patient and gentle nature, in a line carefully bred for cooperation and desire to please. How could I say no?

The biggest catch was that I had to go pick him up, over a hundred miles away. I eyed my ragtop Jeep with concern.

After talking about my reluctance to drive so far with my friend Cindi, she suggested that I ask her father to drive. I did, and he cheerfully agreed.

He was an impeccable driver: not a slowpoke, but not a speeder, and he noticed everything. I mean *everything*. We had to turn around and go back to look at the turkeys he had spotted in someone's backyard (which turned out to be decoys.)

With his delightful and very patient wife Jean, the trip didn't seem nearly as long as it actually was, and soon we were at Pam's.

Jean perched politely on the edge of a big overstuffed armchair; this turned out to be a good idea when the puppies' mother, Blue, leaped up to give her smooches, knocking her backwards harmlessly into the soft upholstery. Paul and I got right down on the floor with the two puppies left. Pam said one of them was hers, destined for the show circuit, and the other was mine.

At first it didn't matter which pup was which; I was delirious playing with two ten-week-old Golden Retrievers. But then Pam left the room, and the bigger, fuzzier pup followed her, while the other chose to stay with me.

"Pam, which one is mine?" I called out, suddenly needing to know.

"That one," she replied from the other room, and I gathered my new chum up and squeezed him tightly. Typical Golden, he responded to this by wriggling ecstatically and licking my face with his puppy-breath tongue.

"Arthur," I whispered fiercely into his soft, floppy ear. "You're my Arthur."

Opossum Tracks

The other day, while my dog Arthur and I were playing in the woods on a snowy afternoon, he happened across some opossum tracks.

Opossums fascinate me, so I let Arthur follow the trail for some distance, just to see what the possum had been doing. They don't hibernate, but remain awake and active (and hungry!) year 'round.

Our only native marsupial, opossums have hands with opposable thumbs, and a dextrous hallux (foot-thumb) in addition to their strong and supple prehensile tail. Adults have a cute bearlike face, but they are shy and nocturnal, and the ones you startle in your barn or see along the road are not at their best.

Of all the local wildlife that might visit your backyard, opossums are one of the most beneficial. Their favorite foods include rats and mice, slugs and snails, bugs and grubs. They'll also eat pet food left out overnight, but don't worry. Most of the positive points to a possum are things they don't do: they don't attack cats or dogs (preferring to flee, or bluff their way out of encounters); they don't chew or claw things; they're quiet (a happy opossum makes a clicking sound with his tongue); and perhaps most interestingly and importantly, they are highly resistant to rabies, and do not get distemper.

Plus, they are immune to snake venom, and will cheerfully kill and eat snakes, including our local rattlesnakes. So if you don't see any snakes in your yard today, it might be because an opossum ate them last night.

So I had no fear for my golden retriever, if he were to suddenly come face-to-face with the maker of the tracks he followed, but neither did I want for him to terrify one of these charming creatures. Opossums don't choose to "play dead" -- it's an involuntary response to overwhelming fear, and anyone trying to survive in the wild around here has difficulties enough without me and my dog interrupting his life with a panic reflex that would leave him unconscious in the snow for anywhere from a few minutes to an hour or more.

"Arthur, heel," I said, as the young dog thrust his nose beneath a fallen tree. Arthur turned and trotted back to me, eager for a pat on the head and a word of praise., and we headed back to the cabin.

"Heel" is a great catch-all command. It combines Come, Sit, and Stay, and is simple to teach to any dog who likes to eat.

As with most tricks, all you need is a bit of roast beef or bacon, and you'll have your dog's immediate and undivided attention.

(For those who want their dog to obey out of love, not expectation of reward -- food is a quick way to a dog's heart. Once the habit is established and reinforced with praise, a treat becomes an occasional pleasant surprise, not a necessity.)

Whatever you want to teach your dog, it helps to run the idiocy out of him first, with a tennis ball or long walk, until he's exhausted enough to think clearly.

To teach a dog to walk at heel, start in a distraction-free, enclosed place, such as the living room. Do not put a leash on the dog; the idea is to outwit him, not initiate a pulling contest. Show the dog a morsel of meat in your left hand. Close your hand loosely around the treat, and with your arm hanging comfortably at your side, invite him to lick the goodie through your fingers.

Now say, calmly and quietly, "Heel," and slowly walk forward. In all likelihood, the dog will also walk forward, with his head by your leg, in the perfect heel position. Control the head and the body follows. Continue to let him nibble the treat as you make turns, repeating "Heel" periodically. Replace the treat as necessary. Encourage him with soft words, such as "good puppy" (regardless of age).

Stop, and without giving any command other than the fact that you stopped, hold the treat above and slightly behind the dog's head. The most comfortable way for him to continue to lick at the treat is to sit. When he does, immediately praise him and let him have whatever's left in your hand.

Just before you start forward again, say, "Heel."

Repeat until you run out of goodies, or fifteen minutes, whichever comes first. Remember, a dog has no idea how large a treat is; he will inhale without chewing whatever you give him, whether it's a crumb the size of your fingernail or an entire sirloin steak.

When he does well in the house, take him outside, WITH a leash, but let the leash hang slack. The treat will pull the dog into position. The leash is only for safety, in case he gets distracted by a squirrel or something.

Eventually when you say, "Heel," your dog will come running to push his nose into the palm of your hand, and you won't even have to glance down to know he's exactly where he belongs.

This method takes awhile (perhaps six months, before you can trust your dog under any circumstances), but once he gets it, the dog won't take advantage when you let him off leash.

As with most ventures, success is directly proportional to time invested. Also, the more you praise your dog, the more eager he will be to earn approval.

Always end every training session on a positive note, and afterwards, play with him! It's good for you both.

Later I went back out, and dropped some treats down the hole the opossum appeared to have commandeered. (They don't dig, but they will move into someone else's burrow, even if the original owner is still in residence. They have been found peacefully coexisting with groundhogs and even badgers.)

I'm sure he appreciated it.

The Cooper's Hawk in the Park

At the park where I often take my golden retriever on lunch hour, some of the nearby houses maintain birdfeeders. In addition to songbirds and squirrels, these feeders also attract several species of raptors. One day, as we approached the fence, I gave Arthur a silent signal to stay, and instead of watching the chickadees at the feeder, I scanned the nearby shrubs.

She was almost invisible, her brown-and-white plumage blending perfectly into the branches and snow: a juvenile Cooper's Hawk staring hungrily at the passerines.

The middle-sized of our three accipiters (ak-SIP-iters) native to Central New York, Cooper's Hawks have short, rounded wings for weaving through trees at high speed, and a long tail to help steer and brake. They make their living by hiding in cover, watching for an unwary bird; then, with a sudden fierce explosion of energy, the hawk darts out and snatches her prey. Often she'll keep going, carrying it off to pluck and devour it in another bit of cover.

Arthur has a bad habit I have yet to solve: as he sometimes does on a long, boring sit-stay, he slid his front feet out and laid down in the snow with a deep doggy sigh of resignation. The nervous Cooper's Hawk took off across the park, heading for a stand of big pines. At sight of the predator, the small songbirds instantly scattered. I stood and watched until the hawk disappeared from view, thinking how lucky we are to live side-by-side with such wonders.

But we hadn't come to the park just to bird-watch.

Pulling my Jeep keys from my pocket, I told Arthur to sit-stay, then wandered out until I was about fifty paces away from him, quietly dropping my keys as I went, then returned to his side. He had caught the sound of the keys and now quivered in place, his floppy ears up as far as they could go, tensely waiting for the command that would release him like a firecracker:

"Arthur, find my keys."

The exuberant puppy shot forward, snuffling along my trail in the snow until he pounced on the key ring. Without hesitation he grasped the icy, jangly metal firmly in his teeth, tossed his head in triumph, and galloped back to me. (Good thing the little flashlight on my key ring is both sturdy and waterproof!) He sat, wagging an arc in the snow, and released the keys when I held out my hand.

"Well done," I said, carefully keeping my voice low and calm. Praising him at this point would send him careening into the ozone with joy, and he hadn't finished this exercise yet.

"At heel," I told him, after he had trembled in place for nearly a minute.

Varying the waiting time prevents "anticipation," where the dog thinks he knows the next command and doesn't wait for the actual words. Not only will this disqualify him in a show, but it's problematic in the real world. For instance, if you want to pull the burdocks off him before he leaps up on you and your hand-knit sweater.

At the words, Arthur whirled around behind me, gave a little hop in a flashy show of enthusiasm, and dropped to sit precisely where he belonged at my left side.

Pocketing the keys, I crouched down and hugged him tight. "You. Are. EXcellent!" I whispered into his silky ear.

Instantly transformed from quiet obedience to lunatic excitement, he grabbed my sleeve, and jumped up on me, wagging his whole self, soaking my coat and jeans in Eau de Wet Dog. (Later my boss would ask, "What's that smell?")

Find My Keys is fairly easy to teach, especially if your dog already retrieves toys, and it can come in handy here in the Snow Belt. My first golden, Arthur's uncle, once found some stranger's set of keys in the plowed snow at the edge of a parking lot. He delivered them to me with justifiable pride, and I turned them over to the owner of the building, who said that a woman had lost her keys a week earlier.

(Hobby could also find and retrieve my glasses, which is another useful talent, because without them I can't find much of anything. However, I can't recommend encouraging an enthusiastic puppy to grab your glasses, unless you have a spare pair.)

The hardest part is getting your dog to pick up metal. The secret? Feed the dog with a metal spoon. I used ravioli, giving them to Arthur one by one from a spoon, and he quickly became used to the feel of metal against his teeth. (A few ravioli won't kill a dog, but I don't suggest it as a steady diet.)

If it horrifies you to share a spoon with your dog, designate one specifically for him. My friend keeps one mug set aside just for me, because I let her beagles share my tea.

Next, play fetch with the spoon. Once your dog doesn't mind retrieving a spoon, toss your keys onto the middle of the living room floor, and continue the game of fetch with them, saying, "Find my keys" every time you throw them.

When your dog brings them back, reward and praise him.

After several sessions, make him sit-stay, and put your hand over his eyes while you toss them into a corner; he'll pinpoint them by sound, and finding them will be easy. When he masters that, take him outside (on a long leash) and let him see you toss your keys into a few inches of snow or grass, depending on the season (making sure you can find them in case he doesn't.) Chances are, he'll bring them to you on the first try. It's that simple.

Dogs Are Learning Every Second They're With You

The other morning, while I was trying to coax my Jeep into starting at minus two degrees, I noticed one of my favorite things about winter in Central New York: sundogs.

Rainbows are the result of sunlight refracting through water droplets; they appear opposite the sun in the sky. Sundogs are the ice crystal version. When it's very cold, and atmospheric conditions are exactly right, there is one sundog on each side of the morning or evening sun, starting around the level of the sun and curving down to the horizon. Magical partial rainbows in the winter sky, sundogs seem to be one of Nature's ways of mitigating bitter cold with beauty.

Maybe the sundogs influenced the Jeep, because it finally caught and sputtered to life -- another triumph for the thirty-two-year-old vehicle.

These last two years have been especially hard on the poor little CJ5. When my golden retriever was a very small puppy, he traveled in a crate in the back of the Jeep, but he outgrew that, and now enjoys riding on the wooden pallet where the back seat used to be, as his uncle before him did.

(There are inherent dangers to having a loose dog in a moving vehicle, but Arthur quietly stays where he belongs, and doesn't push or pester me.)

One of the drawbacks to this arrangement is leaving him for extended periods of time alone in the Jeep. There's a bucket of water and plenty of toys; however, like most puppies, he prefers to chew anything but the items provided for that purpose. Only recently, as Arthur approaches his second birthday, has the damage begun to taper off. His victims include the gearshift knob, the steering wheel (I never knew it had a steel armature inside), and anything removable, like the cigarette lighter.

Even the registration sticker didn't escape his notice. When I approached the desk at the Department of Motor Vehicles and quietly confessed that my dog ate my registration, the clerk gleefully announced this information to the entire room. After laughing at me, they issued a new registration sticker (for a fee, of course), and I plastered it to the window with a large piece of clear tape, which I fervently hoped tasted Awful.

His love of paper is entirely my own fault, of course. When Arthur was only twenty pounds, a friend's husband thought it would be amusing to menace the fuzzy puppy with a newspaper. When I saw my beloved companion cringe, I vowed that he would never, *never* fear a newspaper again. That night when we got home, I collected a pile of old newspapers, and sat down on the floor with my two-month-old retriever. I laughed, and playfully tapped him with a rolled-up paper, until he lost his fear and began to grab the item he'd been hit with.

I praised him and played tuggie with the papers until were were happily rolling on the floor in a drift of shredded newspaper.

Satisfaction came months later when that same guy told Arthur in a bantering tone, "Watch out, or I'll take a rolled-up newspaper to you."

I told him to go ahead.

Barely had the newspaper hit Arthur's shoulder before he yanked the paper from the surprised guy's hand and ripped it into a million pieces, delighting in the destruction.

So today, when Arthur shreds some important document, I have only myself to blame. Every moment you interact with your dog, you're teaching him something, either deliberately or accidentally.

Another thing to consider: When training your dog, you have maybe five seconds to reward or punish behavior. Longer than that, and the dog has moved on to sniffing the carpet or some other innocent pastime, and won't connect your anger with the fact that he ate your TV remote ten seconds ago.

They live very much in the present, and even showing him the mangled remote will not jog his memory.

Shoving a dog's nose in a housetraining indescretion hours after the fact is not only disgusting and unhygienic, but confuses the dog as well.

(An old training axiom: Keep a rolled-up newspaper handy in every room of the house, and when your dog does something that annoys you, immediately grab the nearest paper and swat yourself over the head with it, saying "Bad trainer! Bad trainer!")

One thing I very deliberately taught Arthur from the first day I brought him home: he is not allowed to jump out of the Jeep (or any vehicle.) At first, he was too small anyway, so he got into the habit of letting me pick him up and set him on the ground. Today he weighs more than seventy-five pounds, and can effortlessly jump into the driver's seat nearly four feet off the ground; but he still has no idea that he is physically capable of jumping down.

He patiently waits for me to lift him out, no matter how long it takes me to unload groceries, even when I leave the Jeep door open and disappear into the house. The obvious advantage is that he won't ever leave the Jeep without permission -- a safety measure, because I can't trust the (slightly chewed) door latches of the capricious little Jeep. Another reason is that while jumping up is good exercise for him, the jarring impact of jumping down can damage a large dog's shoulders over the years.

As an added benefit of this daily weightlifting, I can now pick up and walk off with seventy-five pounds, which sure comes in handy when buying dog food.

Maple Syrup

Having hidden a leather glove in the snowy woods the night before, I took my golden retriever out to see if he could follow my tracks and retrieve it after twelve hours. With luck, none of the local wildlife had made off with it in the dark.

"Arthur, find," I said, pointing to the place where I had started out.

Eagerly he snuffled about in the dead leaves just starting to show through the snow, and headed off unerringly, following the same path I had taken. In moments he pounced upon the glove, and as I yelled, "EXcellent!" he brought it back at full speed for praise and petting, which I gladly gave. Then the season and the trees around us gave me a sudden idea, and instead of lying down until the feeling passed (as I should have), I decided to do it.

If you live in the Northeast and have trees in your backyard, the advent of spring may tempt you to try boiling down your own maple syrup, at least once.

First you need the tap, a nifty little thingy that goes into the tree, available seasonally at most local farm stores. Usually I take Arthur with me into the store, but because he's so wildly popular (and I do mean *wildly*), it often takes an extra half hour on top of whatever shopping I need to do. That evening, I left him in the Jeep so we could get home before dark.

What I bought consisted of a stainless-steel spigot part (the "spile"), plus an oddly shaped hook -- assembly required, with no instructions. After fiddling with these obviously incompatible pieces for a few minutes, I gave up and handed the puzzle over to the assistant manager, who with maddening ease and cheerfulness, slid the pieces together for me.

Next you need a bucket. Photos of sugaring operations show gleaming metal buckets with hinged lids; but do they have them at the same store that sells the spiles? Of course not. But really, any clean bucket will do, and a piece of plastic held in place with binder clips will keep out most of the debris and insects.

Then you have to choose a tree. Sugar maples are best (hence the name, haha), but any maple tree can produce syrup. Maple trees are readily identified in summer by their distinctive five-lobed leaf, like the one on the Canadian flag. In mid-March, who can tell?

Trying to remember what type of leaves I saw where last fall, I wandered around in the backyard for awhile, debating. Delighted to accompany me, Arthur danced alongside, begging to carry something.

Deciding on the screwdriver as the least dangerous and most resilient item I had with me, I offered it to him, and he proudly padded around with it, satisfied.

After some deliberation, I selected a big tree that had a two-foot swath of bare wood showing where the bark had been removed somehow, so my hacking a hole in it wouldn't make much of a difference, morally speaking.

Lacking a cordless drill, long extension cord, or even a manual -type drill, I was reduced to using a standard screwdriver and a hammer. (Pro tip: Never let your dog carry around a screwdriver you plan to misuse as a wood chisel. Dog drool makes the end of the handle slippery, and the hammer will slide off and bash your fingers.)

Eventually I had a hole in the tree. After pounding the spile in, I suspended the bucket beneath, affixing its makeshift garbage-bag roof on last.

Sap soon started dripping into the bucket, thup-thup-thup. At the sound, Arthur halted in his tracks and tilted his head quizzically.

I could practically see what he was thinking. In his entire two years of life, every unusual item he had ever seen in the woods had earned him praise when he retrieved it. Arthur took a tentative step toward this novel, noisy item. Quickly I called him to me and we went back inside the house, before he did anything I'd regret.

When the temperatures soared into the mid-thirties, I collected about five gallons of sap (hopefully maple) to convert into a time-honored delicacy.

You can't just park a pot of sap on the woodstove and ignore it for a few days. You must boil it down quickly, or it turns into bitter black goo on the bottom of your best soup pot. (Don't ask.) Another important point: Experts say if you undertake this adventure inside your home, you run the risk that the huge quantities of steam may peel off wallpaper, or even loosen a plaster ceiling.

With these dire warnings in mind, I chose the front porch for our festivities.

I found that a propane camp stove works well -- maybe too well. For the last hour I had to stand right there, freezing in the dark with a flashlight despite the steam fogging up my glasses, to move the pot off the flame whenever the golden bubbles threatened to boil over.

Ah, but the final triumph was sweet indeed: a single cupful of ambrosia, rendered all the more delicious by the pleasure of personal achievement. I poured it into a clean jelly jar and proudly admired it.

Then I discovered that the overspray had made the porch floor sticky. As I idly wondered whether the ants or the bees would get to it first, Arthur came to the rescue. Eyes closed in bliss, he licked the floor clean, suprised when I praised him afterwards.

What a good puppy.

Arthur Discovers that a Golden Retriever can also be a Sled Dog

Arthur's uncle Hobbes used to help me in the winter by dragging firewood up the quarter-mile driveway with a plastic sled. Golden retrievers are famous for their obsessive desire to help their humans, and Hobby was a textbook example, throwing every ounce of his thoroughbred body and soul into the task. His help and companionship made a fun game of what would otherwise have been an onerous nightly chore. But his nephew Arthur just turned three years old on February fourteenth -- in the full early prime of life and vigor -- and until last Saturday, he had never been hitched to a sled.

The main reason I hadn't bothered to teach Arthur to pull a sled is that in the last few years, I've wised up and gotten all my firewood delivered before the first snowfall. That way, the kind gentleman who brings it can get all the way up to my front yard, instead of dumping three cords of split wood down by the road after the driveway has become impassable with drifted snow. Without a compelling motive to hike up and down the driveway in snowshoes, in single-digit temperatures and howling winds, I prefer to spend my evenings curled up by the woodstove with a good book and hot chocolate.

But when my antique Jeep recently decided to take a week-long vacation at the mechanic's, I was reduced to begging rides from friends, then sledding any necessities up to the house, since very few vehicles can get up the narrow track in the woods without either getting scratched up or stuck.

Since the sled had been pulled out of retirement anyway, and I still had Hobby's old harness hanging behind the scarves and jackets on the coat rack, I decided that it was time to introduce Arthur to the sled.

Stuffing a handful of cheese cubes into my coat pocket, I gathered up the harness and the two long nylon leashes, then invited Arthur out into the snow.

Smelling the treats, he danced around in anticipation of earning them, getting snow in my boots.

"Arthur, stand," I told him, and with Herculean effort, the eighty-pound puppy sobered enough to hold still (except for his tail, of course) while I slid the harness on and clipped one leash to either side of it, then ran the lines back to the sled. Once he was hitched up, I tossed a couple pieces of wood into the sled to give it some weight and stability, then told Arthur to stay.

Slogging through the thigh-deep snow, I counted off about twenty paces, then turned and appraised my dog. Arthur stood, wagging with pleasure at this new game, totally unaware of his statuesque beauty as the winter sunlight turned his wavy coat to molten gold.

Speaking in a low and quiet voice in an attempt to convey calmness, I said, "Arthur, come."

Immune to any attempt to calm him, Arthur instantly transformed into a furry whirlwind, plowing through the fluffy snow -- for the first three or four bounds. Then, feeling the tug of the traces, he whipped around to confront whatever was behind him, tangling the lines, which only confused him further.

"Arthur, stay." I untangled the leashes and rearranged everything so the dog was once more in front of the sled. Again I put some distance between us, and gently called him.

Not for nothing is Arthur's pedigree peppered with red-letter champions.

This time he didn't startle at the sled inexplicably following him, and he bounded through the deep snow all the way up to me, wagging hard with excitement.

I should have paid attention to that tail, but I was so pleased with him that without thinking, I gripped his ruff with both hands and praised him: "Excellent! You. Are. EXcellent!!" and fed him all the (now slightly linty) cheese.

Well, that did it. Arthur jumped and twisted in glee, getting snow on my glasses as well as in my boots. The sled, still moving, slid into his back feet, but he was so high on success and praise that he barely noticed. By the time he could think clearly enough to stand still, the six-foot leashes that tied the sled to him were a Gordian knot. I unclipped them at his harness, took the harness off and tossed the whole mess into the sled to figure out later.

Just to tease him, I tossed a snowball into the yard, confident that he wouldn't be able to find a snowball in a snowdrift -- or be willing to pick it up in his teeth, and bring it back intact, even if he could find it.

Wrong on all three counts. He spent a glorious half hour or so retrieving snowballs, until eventually when he stood waiting for me to throw another, he held up one front foot as he panted and wagged.

No whine of complaint accompanied the gesture, but I knew the pain had to be impressive to wring even that minimal acknowledgement from him. He had ice balls between his toes; it was time to go in. Besides, I was soaked through and freezing, anyway. I picked out most of the offending ice and coaxed him back inside.

After the snow melted into puddles on the floor and Arthur was deep in the satisfied sleep of the exhausted, I trimmed the fur between his toes down close, patted his side, and told him he was a good puppy. He thumped the floor with his tail without opening his eyes, and went back to his doggy dreams.

Chipmunks

The first hint I had of the mess I'd have to deal with came in the form of a charming chipmunk (that's a redundancy, I know) busily stuffing sunflower seeds into his cheek pouches on one of the feeders by my kitchen window.

Chipmunks, common and bold daytime rodents here in Central New York, don't hibernate like bears. In addition to putting on a layer of fat, they also spend most of the summer and autumn provisioning their burrow with seeds, nuts, and berries. When the days shorten and the weather turns cold, they go into torpor: their body temperature, heart rate, and breathing drop drastically to conserve energy, but they wake every few days to eat. If the temperatures turn toasty enough (like those fifty-degree days we had in January), they sometimes emerge to forage for food outside.

Except for a mother with young, chipmunks live alone, although their territories often overlap. At least two different chipmunks consider my feeder their personal all-you-can-carry buffet. To keep the chickadees and other songbirds fed, I have to fill the feeders every morning and evening.

I've often thought it would be easier on all of us if I just dumped a bag of sunflower seeds down the neat two-inch-wide hole at the base of my chimney -- but my payment for what the chipmunks take is the pleasure I derive watching them and their high-speed antics.

So when I saw the little chippie, I smiled because he's adorable, and it was nice out. I forgot that warm temperatures also mean mud.

When it comes to mud, there are two types of dogs: those who fastidiously walk around the mud, and those who squelch right through, oblivious of the fact that they've just doubled their weight.

Both of the Australian shepherds I've had were of the former type; both golden retrievers, of the latter. Perhaps it's considered a good trait for a hunting dog to not mind getting wet and dirty. At any rate, when I let my young golden retriever back in that morning, Arthur left big muddy paw-prints all over my wood floor. To make matters worse, it was entirely my own fault.

With a sigh, I knelt and scrubbed. Time to trim Arthur's feet again.

I try to keep the bottoms of his feet clipped close, especially in the winter. Left untrimmed, the fur between the toes of a long-haired dog can create painful ice balls in the tender place between his pads when he walks in snow. When he walks in mud, it doesn't hurt the dog in the slightest, but that extra fur works like a sponge, sopping up huge quantities of mud to be smeared all over the floor later. I called Arthur over.

One test of how much your dog trusts you: tell him to sit-stay, then you sit on the floor direcly behind him, with your ankles on either side of him. Gently pull him over backwards onto your legs, with his head in your lap. If he lets you do this without struggling, he's confident in you and content with his social standing. (If he doesn't, it's something to work on.)

It's also the simplest way I've found to clip nails and trim foot-fur.

Arthur, like his uncle Hobby did, lays quietly in the trough of my legs, and I can take my time with the nail-trimmers and scissors. Besides being an excruciating surprise when your dog dances on your stocking feet (as dogs are wont to do), overlong nails can impede a dog's stride by forcing the toes to turn unnaturally sideways.

The trick is to cut enough, but not too much. With a dog who has clear nails, trimming down to the quick (the vein inside the nail) is relatively easy; black nails are a bit harder. If you look closely, you can see where the underside of the nail turns spongy in the center. Do not cut into that.

It's safest to do each nail in a series of nibbles, rather than taking just one big bite with the trimmers, so it's very helpful if the dog just lays there patiently.

The ideal time to clip nails is before dinner but after you've exercised your dog to exhaustion, not at two AM when you're sleep-dazed and groggy, with a flashlight between your teeth, and he's been wide-awake and antsy for an hour (or however long it took for the click-click-clicking to wrench you from bed before you went mad, utterly mad.) This way your canine chum comes to the project with his maximum attention span, and afterwards you can use dinner as a reward -- the tried-and-true recipe for a positive training experience.

Also, it's worth noting that you should also try to only clip your dog's nails while you're wearing scruffy jeans and a t-shirt, and don't mind getting a little dirty. It seems a bit pointless to take a nice long, hot shower with rose-scented soap, spray on a little cologne and slide into your best set of silky pajamas, only to crawl out of your nice warm bed a little while later to go sit on the floor with a lapful of dog who hasn't had a bath in weeks.

When you start snipping with scissors at the fur between his toes, it's definitely safer for both of you if the dog doesn't pull or fuss. Rub his tummy. Give him a quiet and calm "good puppy," to encourage him to continue laying still. (This is far different from the "EXcellent!" shout of praise that releases him.) Alternate petting and trimming. Make it fun.

Arthur loves getting his feet done. As usual, he laid there in my lap, eyes closed and tail sweeping the floor drowsily, while I cut his nails, filed the sharp edges off, and scissored the fur as close as I could get between his toes. Then, inexplicably, I lost my head and clipped away the tufts of fur on top of his feet as well, rounding his toes off like the pictures in the breed journals.

Last spring at the Golden Reunion, they laughed at what they called Arthur's "Dr. Seuss feet." They even offered to trim him down like a show dog right then and there. But I was adamant, and he came home with his foot-fur intact.

I don't know what possessed me to finally try the show clip instead of his customary casual fuzzy look, but now Arthur looks like he's prancing tippy-toe on little nubbins of feet.

Unfortunately, I can only wait for this formal show-dog look to grow out, or grow on me. Arthur, of course, couldn't care less.

Arthur Helps with a Monarch Butterfly Project

On my way into town the other day, I was surprised to see my friend Mary picking weeds by the roadside. Curiosity piqued, I stopped and got out. To Arthur's supreme disappointment, I left him in the Jeep because I wasn't quite sure what was going on. As it turns out, that was a good decision, because in his delight he would have unwittingly stomped to death the critters Mary was intent on collecting. So Arthur stood on the driver's seat and leaned out as I approached Mary and asked what she was doing.

With a grin, Mary shifted the weeds to her other hand and opened the container she was carrying, explaining that she was picking milkweed for her caterpillars. In the deli cup she had several Monarch caterpillars, their vibrant yellow, white and black vertical stripes bright against the leaves they were busily chewing.

Brimming with enthusiasm, she said, "This has been a great year for caterpillars. Usually we only get one or maybe two on a plant, but this year we've been finding three or four."

Inferring that she has kept caterpillars before, I asked how one goes about keeping these nifty larvae healthy and happy enough to watch them turn into the beautiful black and orange butterflies.

She said it wasn't that difficult. All you have to do is provide a caterpillar-proof enclosure (Mary suggested a ten-gallon aquarium) and milkweed. A very common plant, milkweed is easily identified by its wide, oval leaves, exotic pink flowers, and odd-shaped seed pods filled with fluff, in addition to the namesake milky juice that comes out of the stem when cut.

Milkweed is the monarch caterpillar's sole source of nutrition, and the toxins in the plant accumulate in the caterpillar's body, rendering the adult butterfly poisonous to predators, as its vivid coloration proclaims. (The edible Viceroy butterfly takes advantage of this by mimicking the Monarch's pattern.)

Mary, an experienced butterfly enthusiast, places the stems of the harvested milkweed in a glass of water to keep the leaves fresh, careful to cover the water with netting to prevent the caterpillars from falling in and drowning.

Set the habitat on a counter or outside (not in direct sunlight, or you'll have fried caterpillars) and let Nature do the rest. Eventually, each caterpillar will strip itself down to a green chrysalis and pupate into the familiar butterfly, at which point they can be released, none the worse for passively providing a glimpse inside the fascinating world of insects. (A chrysalis is a hard-shelled pupa; a cocoon is layers and layers of spun silk enveloping a pupa.)

Eager to share this experience, a few days later I parked by a patch of milkweed and went out in search of caterpillars. Perhaps taking a container along might have been a good idea; I ended up carrying several milkweed stalks back to the Jeep, where I was compelled to put them in my cooler along with dinner, lest Arthur inhale the smaller caterpillars in his never-ending quest for nasal knowledge.

Monarchs only remain caterpillars for about two weeks, so it wasn't long before one fine fat fellow glued himself to the top of the enclosure and hung there, curled up and motionless, for half a day. Unfortunately I missed seeing him shrug out of his skin. The next time I looked, there was a translucent leaf-green chrysalis with the discarded skin at the top, rolled up like a snake shed. After a day or so, the chrysalis hardened and the signature metallic gold ornamentation appeared. Now I just had to wait ten days.

Monarchs go through several generations each summer, most only living a few weeks. But the ones that emerge here in the autumn will spend the winter as far south as Mexico; they are one of the few insects that migrate. These monarchs live several months, returning tattered and worn to lay eggs here in the spring and start the cycle all over.

Arthur thoroughly enjoyed the daily forays for fresh milkweed, although when he insisted on helping carry one of the cut pieces, he quickly spit it out with a sharp snort and shake of his head. Still, there's plenty for a retriever to do in a weedy field, especially since the farmer who owns the field on the other side of the road recently turned loose dozens of captive-bred pheasants. Inevitably, some of the birds found their way to my side, ignoring my "No Trespassing" signs.

Once all the caterpillars had turned into chrysalises, I took them up to my friend Lucille's house so she could enjoy seeing the butterflies emerge without enduring the mess and smell of frass (I kid you not, this is the technical term for caterpillar poop.) After about a week and a half, the casings turned clear and started showing the colors of the mature insect inside. One by one the butterflies split open their prisons then stood around, slowly opening and closing their black-and-orange wings, stretching and drying them.

After observing them for awhile and taking pictures, I told Arthur to leave them *alone,* and we reverently released them, wishing them luck on their arduous journey.

Thanks, Mary!

A Dog by a Different Name Might Respond Better

When I was a kid and my mother used my full name, I knew I was in trouble. This, like many other behavior-modification methods, works equally well with dogs as with children. My first Golden Retriever's real name was Hobbes, but I only called him that when he'd done something really wrong, which was rare. He had a handful of nicknames, endearments really -- Ashka, Ash, Cash, Vachon -- and the only confusion produced by this plethora of names was among his various human aquaintances.

Arthur, too, is accustomed to answering to an assortment of names. If he's just done something supremely stupid, like grabbing a toy he knows isn't his, I call him Jerk in mild admonishment. He hears this name less frequently now that he's outgrown the idiocy of puppyhood. But when I call him Artos, Wolftracks, or (inaccurately) Mutt, he's confident that I'm pleased with him, which is his main goal in life.

It might sound crazy to give a dog several names, but it's actually a terrific training tool. Generally I use the name "Arthur" to keep his doggy excitement level to a minimum when we go out; I say it in a no-nonsense voice, calm but firm, when he needs to behave sedately: "Arthur. Heel." He knows he absolutely *must* obey, instantly and without question.

But at home or out on trails, when I just want him to check in with me without cutting short whatever fun he's having, I say, "Artos," and he pulls himself out of the weeds, gives me eye contact, then then plunges back in, to add more burdocks to his fluffy coat.

The name "Wolftracks" refers to the giant muddy footprints he makes, and Arthur knows that when I use this name, he's supposed to stand still while I wipe his feet clean. This doesn't by any means keep my house immaculate, but left to his own devices, Arthur would track in enough dirt to grow crops in the kitchen. Since I always praise him lavishly afterwards, he loves this name.

And if I softly call him "Mutt," I should first take off my glasses and brace myself, because he immediately throws his whole seventy-five-pound self ecstatically upon me, panting in my face, his big brushy tail wagging hard.

If you yell, "Rover! Bad dog!" when your dog chews up your checkbook, and then yell, "Rover! Come!" when you want him to return to you, don't be surprised if he hangs back, afraid to approach. (One inviolate rule of dog training: never, *never* punish your dog for coming when you call, no matter what crime he may have perpetrated.)

Luckily, even if your dog has gotten into the habit of not coming when you call, or waiting until you repeat yourself several times, you can start fresh with a different name.

From the outset, you must give the command, enforce it, then reward him, consistently. To get a dog to come, that's usually just a matter of putting a long leash on him, letting him wander around, then calling him once. If he does not instantly gallop over to you, don't give the command again; simply reel him in, then praise him. A bit of ham or roast beef helps him focus. A mistake many people make is to give the same command more than once, and the dog quickly learns he can ignore the first two or three commands, or all of them entirely.

Another tip: don't ask your dog to come; *tell* him (but you don't need to shout like a drill sergeant, either.) Use a calm, confident tone: "Rover, come." Not, "Rover? Come here, boy?" which makes it sound like he has a choice, nor the idiotic, "Rover, good puppy, come here," where he gets praised before doing what you want. What's that going to teach him?

This all becomes of vital practical importance when your dog happens upon a skunk hunting for grubs behind the shed. Unless startled, skunks often tolerate a reasonable amount of canine curiosity, and usually give fair warning before initiating chemical warfare.

If your dog is unfortunate enough to bear the brunt of a skunk's olfactory defensive tactics, you can try the traditional tomato-juice bath, but even better is this simple recipe: one quart of three percent hydrogen peroxide; one quarter cup of baking soda; and one teaspoon of liquid dish soap (which breaks down the oil in the skunk musk.)

This solution has to be mixed up fresh right before use, because the chemical reaction will make it blow the lid off if sealed up (remember those baking soda and vinegar volcanoes?) Soak the dog thoroughly (careful of eyes, nose, and ears), rinse well, finish with a nice floral shampoo, and your dog will be welcome in the house again — at least until the next skunk encounter.

Arthur Meets a Murder of Crows

The other day I took Arthur over to a friend's house, and lifted him out of the Jeep to the ground -- a practice that not only prevents shoulder injuries (to the dog), it keeps him from jumping out on his own. Once on the snowy ground, the big retriever (and he seems to get bigger every time I have to lift him) had to go check the ten-by-ten square patch of lawn where the snow is kept carefully cleared under one of the leafless maple trees.

Bits of stale bread and freezer-burned meat littered the ground temptingly, but Arthur inspected it all with purely academic interest; he has never touched a single piece, ever since I told him to "leave it alone" the first time he discovered it. Uneasily I watched the hungry crows in the tree overhead, who in turn watched the young dog.

Many people, particularly those with a clean-car fetish, abhor these aerial invaders, and go to great lengths to avoid or drive them away. Others admire them as the highly intelligent critters they are, and actively try to attract them, with varying degrees of openness about the practice.

For instance, one of my friends who feeds the crows year round only agreed to let me include them in this article on condition of anonymity. I've seen these crows congregate in the mornings, waiting for my friend to serve their first buffet of the day. It's kind of creepy, and coming from me, that's saying something.

The original intention, I believe, was to prevent the crows from ripping apart the garbage by providing them with yummier alternatives, and as far as that goes, it works. In return for easy, tasty victuals, they refrain from tearing apart the trash. However, with the onset of severe weather, the crow presence escalated from four or five birds to the multitude now milling about, murmuring amongst themselves above my naive retriever.

The collective noun for a group of crows is called a "murder." I called Arthur and we went inside.

My anonymous friend isn't the only one I know who admires the plucky crows, and feeds them in exchange for the pleasure of watching their antics. My Aunt Gerry down in Georgia has a small family of crows who not only visit regularly, they come when she calls them. She simply says, "Crows!" in her delightful Southern accent when she puts tidbits out on the porch, and the crows, having quickly made the connection between this sound and free food, promptly come flying in.

Another friend of mine in Dryden trained some of the local crows to respond to his whistle for buttered bread. Again, he accomplished this quite easily, by always giving a distinctive whistle when he laid out the bread.

Crows aren't just a nuisance, but interesting creatures just trying to survive and raise their families. Cornell's crow expert, Kevin McGowan, has a fascinating first-hand account of his research on crow behavior and intelligence.

One of Nature's most adaptable creatures, crows have embraced the suburban lifestyle, thriving where man has encroached upon their environment. Still, most crows don't even see their first birthday. Those who survive that first decisive winter can live an average of seventeen to twenty-one years. Considered by experts to be among the top of the world's smartest birds, crows generally mate for life, and they maintain close family units. Last year's grown youngsters help their parents raise this year's chicks. They're smart enough to know that even if they aren't hungry right now, they will be later, so they cache food (exactly like humans buying a week's worth of groceries all at once, instead of just that night's dinner.) Their infamous predilection for roosting in cities is probably also due to their intelligence: they've learned that they are safe from guns in the city, and fewer owls hunt there. The artificial light may also help them keep watch for danger even at night.

McGowan has discovered that crows have a charming ability not apparent in most other birds: crows can recognize individual humans. If you offer them food on a regular schedule (he suggests unsalted, unshelled peanuts), they will figure out your routine and wait for you specifically, ignoring other non-food-providing humans. They can even learn to recognize your car, and make a deliberate attempt to attract your attention if you're late with the food.

And it would seem that these folks who feed them have the right idea. Because crows can individualize, you want them to like you. If they come to perceive you as the enemy, they may well harry you at every opportunity, as they do to Great Horned Owls (who are clearly immune to the implications of the adage "eating crow.")

On our way out to the Jeep that day, I let Arthur sniff what was left of the crow food, and said "Hi!" to the big, black birds peering warily down from their perches on the wires. Some of them took off, but the majority stayed.

They've seen me before, and I've never threatened them.

Yes, they make a mess. But crows are here to stay. Try parking elsewhere, or drape a sheet over your car at night; then go ahead, make friends with the crows.

Feed them, and call them by name. I won't tell.

Arthur Chooses Treat Over Dead Eastern Milksnake

Occasionally I take Arthur for a walk instead of sitting on the porch tossing a ball for him (add a bag of marshmallows, and I can actually gain weight exercising my dog.) A good mile-long walk is not only invigorating, it's also a great way to see interesting things.

Of course, you can only enjoy the sights if you don't have to constantly worry about where your dog is. My preferred method is to carry tidbits. All it takes to keep your dog nearby is a handful of treats -- and the yummier the treat, the more likely your dog is to stick to you like a burdock. This doesn't mean he needs to maintain perfect heel position, unless you're walking along a road. On a path or in the brush, I sometimes let Arthur pad about as he wants, because he knows it's his job to keep track of where I am, not the other way around.

Treats, in addition to the chance that I might praise him or pet him, prevent him from wandering and guarantee an instant, galloping response when I call him.

The ultimate signal for Arthur to return to me is when I crouch down with both arms held out wide. When he sees me do that, all else is completely eclipsed, and he races toward me, feet flying, chest low to the ground, and floppy ears flapping, eager for a hug and a smooch.

Most dogs have an innate desire to please; it's part of their psyche as pack animals. Generally, all you have to do is step into the role of leader and they will readily accept you as their dominant packmate, but it is *essential* for you to actively behave like the leader.

It's not enough to passively assume that your dog will identify you as the alpha. With the retriever group, it doesn't take much to convince them, but some other breeds are prone to testing their limits, or even outright challenging for the alpha position. And the hounds, without being deliberately disobedient, might ignore you simply because their nose found something more interesting at the moment than pack loyalty.

Maintaining your status as the pack leader doesn't mean you have to watch for every slightest infraction or enforce your position with physical discipline. You can't force him to respect you; that must be earned. The only thing that hitting your dog will make him do is fear you, and possibly grow aggressive in self-defense. You should be able to outsmart your dog, and if you can't do that, you shouldn't have a dog.

It's easy to establish a few common-sense rules, trick the dog into obeying, then reward him. Food is a powerful tool; use it wisely. For instance, whenever we walk along a road, I insist that Arthur pace sedately beside me, and I taught him to do so by carrying treats in my left hand. Now no treats are necessary, and he walks at heel more out of habit than by command. But sometimes his self-control is tested.

One afternoon while my friend Lucille and I were walking along her quiet country road, we halted to identify a dead Eastern Milksnake. It had apparently chosen to bask on the sun-warmed pavement -- resulting, sadly, in its reduction from three dimensions to two. Although the pathetic corpse had been there for some time drying out in the sun, its distinctive pattern was still clearly visible: tan body with brown ovals outlined in black, with a heart-shaped splotch on top of the head. The underside is a vivid black-and-white checkerboard pattern. A newly-hatched Eastern Milksnake is about the size of a pencil, and this specimen seemed to be about three feet long, probablly a three- or four-year-old snake who would now never achieve his six-foot potential.

Frequently found in barns, milksnakes are so named for the old and erroneous superstition that they suck milk from cows. (I was devasted to discover that Colonel Moran could not possibly have trained a venomous snake to come when called for a reward of a saucer of milk, as Sir Arthur Conan Doyle described in the story, "The Adventure of the Speckled Band." Besides the fact that they don't drink milk, snakes are stone deaf. The closest they come to hearing is feeling vibrations.)

What milksnakes are really doing in barns is hunting rodents -- and other snakes. Our common Eastern Milksnake is one of the kingsnakes, which means that they, like opossums, consider a rattlesnake just another snack. And yes, here in Central New York we do indeed have Timber Rattlesnakes, although they're generally shy and rarely seen, as they blend in well with the forest floor. The surest field mark of a rattlesnake is, obviously, the rattle at the end of its tail; but the rattle can break off, so no rattle does NOT mean it's not venomous. When in doubt, leave it alone.

At my side, Arthur leaned forward to sniff at the dead snake that we humans had shown such interest in. I gingerly tossed the snake off to the side of the road, so as not to tempt other critters to venture out onto the road for a meal. Then Lucille and I continued our walk.

I failed to notice that Arthur didn't come to heel quite as quickly as he customarily does.

He must have thought that leaving the snake behind was an oversight. Plus, I'd thrown it, hadn't I? A deceased and deliciously dried-up reptile -- what's not to like?

A pocketful of treats is also a good way to get your dog to relinquish that several-days-dead snake he just picked up.

A Retriever Can Learn to Get Along with a Chicken

Through no fault of my own, I find myself more or less in possession of a large red rooster. It's a long story, but here he is, and I can't even hope he'll be picked off by the local Great Horned Owl, since he's taken to sleeping on top of the firewood stacked on the porch.

With a wingspan of four to five feet, Great Horned Owls are common anywhere rodents are plentiful, but they often go unnoticed because they hunt mostly at night, and during the day their tree-bark camouflage hides them from all but the sharpest eyes.

Big, powerful birds, the velvety surface of their flight feathers sacrifices speed for silence, giving them the added advantage of surprise; a forty-pound raccoon has no warning before several two-inch-long talons are driven through its skull. Like most birds, Great Horned Owls have nearly no sense of smell, making them one of the few natural predators of skunks. They are capable of not only killing, but picking up and flying off with a skunk twice the owl's own body weight.

Overall, I'd rather the rooster sleep on the firewood; it's a vast improvement over having him sleep on the hood of my antique Jeep. I really don't mind big, messy poops on a hunk of wood I'm tossing into the woodstove, but I did rather object to his Jackson Pollock efforts at providing the Jeep with a hood ornament. Chicken poop is tenacious stuff.

Initially, Arthur greeted the arrival of this flightless bird with the delirious rapture of a retriever bred for hunting wily pheasants. He could have caught and brought the rooster to me easily, for the bird has no fear, and in fact only grudgingly moves out of the way when Arthur races in manic circles around the yard.

"Arthur, leave it alone," I laid the law, just once; this immediately and forever rendered the bird untouchable. Arthur now occasionally sniffs at the rooster curiously, but would no more think of grabbing it than he would eat a plate of spaghetti left on the floor. (Teaching your dog not to eat anything unless you give clear and specific permission is more than just a parlor trick; it could save your dog's life, if he happens upon some rat poison, chicken bones, or anything else dangerous to eat.)

This level of training looks far more impressive than it really is. All you need to start is half a pound of ham (or any type of super-yummy treat), plus a toy-type item that you aren't particularly attached to, such as a dollar-store plushie.

Sit down with your pup, and with one arm around him, show him the toy in a matter-of-fact way, trying not to tease him with it. Say his name in a calm, no-nonsense voice, then "Alone" (or whatever key word you want to use.)

Having no clue what the word "alone" means, he might assume you are offering him the toy, and try to take it. Tell him "no," press the toy lightly against his nose, and repeat the command, "Alone." Pushing the toy toward him is a psychological trick; most dogs will turn their head away from something coming at their face.

Set the toy on the floor in front of both of you, and distract him, petting him and feeding him tidbits, until he is completely ignoring the toy. After awhile, quit petting him and encourage him to get up and move around, but watch him closely -- if he seems at all interested in the toy, pick it up and put it right in front of his nose, repeating, "Alone."

If he does get hold of it, do not attempt to pull it away; that will just lead to a counterproductive game of tuggie.

Tell him to "drop" it (he has long since learned to let go of something when ordered to, yes?) and begin over.

There is a downside to this command, if your dog learns it well. The first dog I taught it to was our miniature poodle, Sassy, when I was in high school. After being told on several occasions to ignore a bowl of cereal left unguarded on the floor (I liked to eat breakfast on the floor while watching Saturday morning cartoons), Sassy needed no reminder to respect my bowl of Froot Loops -- and I never noticed how carelessly I took her good manners for granted until we visited my grandparents one weekend (leaving Sassy in a kennel.)

As usual, I left my bowl of cereal on their living room floor to go get something during a commercial break. When I came back, I could only stand and stare in astonishment as Fluffy, my grandmother's big black poodle, finished licking my bowl clean. She displayed the happy gratitude of one who has thoroughly enjoyed an unexpected windfall, and I didn't even get the satisfaction of reprimanding her, because she was entirely blameless.

Heaven knows any canine guest possessing even the most rudimentary hunting instincts would make short work of my naive red rooster; fortunately for the rooster, doggie visitors are few and far between. And while firewood burns just as well with chicken poop as without, my wood gloves will never be quite the same. I confess this is one instance when it would be easy to forgive Arthur if he happened to forget his training, just for a moment …

Building a Polliwog Pond

Each summer I wind up keeping an aquarium of polliwogs on my porch. Every spring the wood frogs came to lay their eggs in shallow puddles in my yard, not realizing that these would dry up before the tadpoles matured. Every year I felt compelled to rescue them, raise them, then release them.

Wood frogs are common in areas that have both water and -- as their name implies -- woods. The adults are about three inches long, brownish with a white belly, sport a raccoon-like mask, and have a pair of raised lines running from head to rump.

One of the earliest spring breeders, male wood frogs seek out vernal pools (the temporary puddles that form in the spring) and emit a surprisingly loud plea for a girlfriend. After mating, the female wood frog lays a mass of up to a thousand eggs in the water, and the adults return to the woods, where their camouflage hides them from predators as they eat insects, spiders, slugs, snails, and caterpillars, ambushing their prey or actually sneaking up on it. In the winter they hibernate beneath rocks, stumps, and dead leaves. These fascinating amphibians don't even need to dig down below the frostline, because if they freeze solid, they can thaw out without harm.

Maintaining a hundred-odd polliwogs in an aquarium isn't easy. I bought spirulina algae fish flakes to replace the natural algae they should eat, plus I had to keep their container clean, which entailed scooping out most of the water using an old yogurt container, so I could spot any errant little tadpoles against its white interior before I tossed the icky water across the lawn. Then I had to refill the tank with water at the same temperature. All of this had to be done every day, or the water turned cloudy and the tadpoles would start dying off.

As they got older and grew legs, the nascent frogs needed to be able to leave the water periodically before ultimately abandoning their aquatic environment and hopping off into the woods, as wood frogs are supposed to do.

Several hunks of slate laid at a slant in their tank seemed to make them happy, but made cleaning the tank that much more difficult. The answer, I decided, was to put in a small pond; with luck, the local frogs would lay their eggs in the pond instead of the puddles, and I wouldn't have to do anything at all.

Accordingly, one afternoon I assembled what I'd need for the project: a shovel, a piece of durable yet flexible plastic, a heap of slate, and Arthur's bright-orange lacrosse ball.

First, I had to run my young Golden Retriever into exhaustion without exhausting myself -- thus the ball. I stood in the front yard and threw the ball as hard as I could. Arthur gave chase with such enthusiasm that when he closed his jaws on the ball, the rest of him continued on, flipping end-over-end. I couldn't help laughing, and Arthur circled back, heading straight for me like a locomotive, barely swerving aside at the last second.

"Gimme that!" I said, grabbing the ball while it was still between his teeth.

Gleefully Arthur held on. This phrase gives him permission to play tuggie, and like most dogs, Arthur *loves* to play tuggie.

It's a challenge to hang onto a slobbery ball while the dog has the unfair advantage of holding the ball entirely in his mouth, so we alternated between tuggie and fetch, until Arthur flopped down in the shade of a tree, grass-stained and satisfied.

Mentally mapping out a rough oval nearly three feet wide by four feet long in front of the rosebushes, I dug a hole about eighteen inches deep in the center, sloping the edges so baby frogs could get in and out easily. Then I laid the plastic down, tucked the edges beneath slabs of slate, filled the pond with about forty gallons of water, and trimmed it off prettily on one side with some wild wood violets.

After surveying my handiwork with pride for several moments, I shouldered the shovel and headed back toward the house -- only to halt at the sound of slurping.

Arthur, rested up from his earlier antics, was quenching his thirst in the new pond, literally: he was laying down in the water as he drank. Fortunately, the liner survived.

After removing the canine and letting the water warm up for a few hours, I gently dumped in the current (and hopefully last) tank of polliwogs. I still had to feed them until the pond acquired its own natural algae, but I didn't have to clean it, or worry about them not being able to leave when they wanted to. It worked wonderfully.

This spring, I had every intention of cleaning the fallen leaves and winter gunk out of the pond, but the wood frogs were too quick for me, demonstrating their approval of my handiwork by depositing three fist-sized masses of eggs. Would cleaning the pond now disturb them? I didn't know, and didn't dare risk it.

The good news is that as they get larger, polliwogs eat insects and larvae as well as algae -- so although the pond looks more primoridal than ornamental, at least it's not breeding mosquitoes.

Enjoying Halloween with Good-Natured Arthur

Halloween has always been one of my favorite holidays: dressing up my dog, showing him off, and best of all, eating vast amounts of chocolate without feeling guilty for not sharing, because chocolate is bad for dogs.

As little as one ounce of baking chocolate, one eight-ounce bar of dark chocolate, or one pound of milk chocolate can be enough to poison a forty-pound dog.

The first symptoms include excitability, panting, vomiting, tremors, diarrhea and incontinence. Caught early enough, your canine chum might survive theobromine poisoning if taken immediately to a veterinarian. Untreated, the later stages are seizures, coma, and death.

Still, chocolate is a Halloween tradition. This year, as usual, I purchased my favorite type, just in case I'm "stuck" eating it all myself. I also got a cute plastic jack-o-lantern bucket with a handle for Arthur to hold in his

mouth, and a terrific devil costume for him, complete
with red satin cape. I even splurged on a silly green witch
hat for myself, with frizzy lime-green hair.

Ah, I was prepared! I'd put the outfit on Arthur, and
have him sit in the doorway holding the bucket of candy
when the kids knocked. How cute would that be?

On Halloween night, I came straight home from
work and turned the porch light on, illuminating the
festive cornstalks, pumpkins, and gourds on the porch
steps. Then, just as I was taking my coat off, there was a
knock on the door! Our first! But I wasn't ready yet!

Arthur barked excitedly as I rushed to open a package
of candy, dump it into the plastic pumpkin bucket, and
answer the door my plain old un-cute self. I didn't even
remember to grab my witch hat.

An adorable little girl in a red butterfly costume
smiled shyly and said, "Trick or treat!"

She got a candy bar and left, her parents following her.

Quickly I slid the devil costume on Arthur, and
with equal parts coaxing and pizza crust, convinced
him to leave it on. Finally he gave in and accepted this
uncomfortable outfit, merely because he understood that
I wanted him to, in typical *Golden Retriever* fashion.

Next, I showed him the bucket, with five chocolate
bars still inside it. I held it in front of him and said,
"Arthur, take it."

I've asked Arthur to retrieve buckets before.
Immediately, he reached across the top to grab the far
edge, having learned from experience that picking up

a bucket by the closest edge left him looking into the bucket, unable to see where he was going.

He reached, but I slid the handle between his jaws instead, repeating the process until he figured out that I wanted him to hold this bucket by the handle.

Finally, there he sat, holding it proudly, his fluffy golden tail swishing an arc on the floor behind him. I took the bucket and handed him a delicious sliver of beef.

Then I hung the witch hat next to the door, filled the bucket with more candy, and set it on the bookshelf, safely beyond reach of anyone shorter than me (I'm only five foot one, but still taller than any of the household's four-footed folk.) Then I waited for our next costumed visitor.

And waited. And waited. Two hours went by. Nothing. Nada. Zip.

Disappointed, at eight-thirty I finally admitted that we weren't going to get any more than that one trick-or-treater, shut off the porch lights, and put the candy away.

With great disappointment and reluctance I pulled the devil costume off a visibly grateful Arthur, and rewarded him for his patience with his usual dinner of kibble. I also praised and petted him, which of course made Arthur ecstatic, but it made me feel better, too. Funny how that works.

We still had seventeen bars of delicious chocolate. I will keep Arthur safe from theobromine poisoning by eating all this leftover Halloween candy myself. I'm thoughtful like that.

Arthur Hears an Eastern Screech Owl

The other night when I took Arthur out, I heard a rather spooky sound, probably a bird, maybe an owl? I grabbed my camera (the only recording device at hand) and hurried back out, pausing only to scuff into my lawnmowing sneakers.

The spine-chilling, plaintive wail ended with a sort of whinny as it trailed off. Over and over it repeated, at about thirty-second intervals. Carefully I recorded it, aiming my camera into the darkness of the tall pines behind the house.

Arthur clearly considered this impromptu outing a happy excuse to run around the lawn and sniff the grass for interesting scents, completely at ease with the odd sounds. He has no fear of anything.

I knew from experience that some of our local owls can make surprisingly loud sounds despite their diminutive size -- some of them eerily humanlike. Whatever this was, it almost seemed to be laughing at my dog and me.

After about ten minutes, the mesmerizing cries began to grow softer, as if their maker started moving away, and I suddenly realized I was freezing, standing there in my pajamas. Back we retreated into the warm house and the incredible convenience of vast amounts of easily-accessible information, a.k.a., the internet.

The Owl Foundation, based in Canada, offers crystal-clear audio files of several different vocalizations made by our common Eastern Screech Owl. After comparing theirs to what I had just recorded, our strange guest now had a name and a wide-eyed, adorable face to go with the uncanny calls.

Often mistaken for a baby owl, adult Eastern Screech Owls stand barely six inches high, and weigh only four to nine ounces. (Baby owls can be any size from nestling Saw-Whet Owls that would fit three to a coffee mug, to Great Horned Owls with a five-foot wingspan.) Regardless of size, baby owls are easily identified as such by grayish fuzzy down feathers sticking out at odd angles, like Albert Einstein on a bad hair day.

Screech owls, although common and tending to nest and hunt near human habitations because of the availability of prey, often go unnoticed. Their mottled plumage, long "ear" tufts, and habit of standing up tall and straight all help them blend almost invisibly into the trees where they sleep all day.

Eastern Screech Owls hunt mostly insects and small nocturnal rodents, and each owl can eat one or two mice per night. This makes them valuable to farmers as a free form of pest control.

Once the mystery of our interloper's identity was satisfactorily solved, I called it a night, and I curled up in bed with a book, and with Arthur pressed against my side, his bearlike (drooly) head across my stomach. Where he belongs.

Arthur Meets the Challenge of Tracking the Right Person

One tracking test I had yet to give Arthur: two people, both strangers to him, go into the woods together, and then split up. The dog's job is to find the person whose scent he was given, without becoming distracted by the second person -- much more complicated than simply following one trail.

I was curious if Arthur could do it, but had so far lacked the necessary multiple simultaneous visitors. Happily, my neighbors recently came over, and Arthur had not yet met them.

Even better, they're experienced with working dogs; Mary's beagles do agility trials with great success, despite the fact that beagles are not the most popular breed for this growing sport.

Excited, I shut Arthur in the house, and waited outside on the porch in the cold.

Mary and her friend soon arrived, and cheerfully agreed to lay a track in the woods for Arthur.

"Don't go too far," I cautioned, as the young lady handed me her knit hat and set off into the pines, with her friend close behind. I wasn't worried about them in the woods, nor Arthur's ablity to follow a long trail; nope, I was thinking of how Arthur drags me through the woods at top speed, and I can only try to keep up as best I can, because I don't want to give him commands of any sort while he's tracking. The whole idea is for the dog to lead the way.

As they laughed and wandered around in the blackberry patch, I went in the house to get Arthur and give them time to get a decent distance away. While I waited, I watched the lively chickadees at the feeder.

Black-capped chickadees are a beloved common visitor to birdfeeders. For this species, human encroachment has been a boon, except where habitat destruction is too severe. In the summer, chickadees obtain protein from all sorts of invertebrates, including spiders, slugs, snails and insects of every kind, often pinning down their prey with their feet while they eat. In the winter they are dependent upon seeds and the occasional berry for sustenance, caching some of what they find for later.

Their call is the namesake "chickadee-dee-dee" and their song is a clear, whistled "see-me, see-me," the first note higher than the second, as they sit in plain sight on a branch. According to Cornell, these deceptively short sounds are actually intricate enough for individuals to identify others as belonging to the same or different flocks -- but I expect that only another chickadee can fully understand the nuances.

Unlike many small birds, chickadees do not display sexual dimorphism -- in other words, both genders look alike, with their black cap and bib, white cheeks, gray back, and buffy sides. To add to the confusion of their human audience, once fledged, immature birds look exactly like their parents.

Petting Arthur, I watched one chickadee take a fast and messy bath in the bowl I put out for them; then I figured we had waited long enough for Mary and her friend to finish hiking and get settled.

I put the harness and heavy leash on Arthur. He immediately knew what was up, and I had to laugh at his eagerness. Carefully keeping Mary's hat beneath my coat, I took Arthur outside, where he dropped his nose to the ground, all set to search, his tail wagging so hard he hit his sides.

It wouldn't be much of an indication of the dog's tracking skill if he heard them walking around, so I stopped and stood for a moment, listening. When I was satisfied that the woods were silent, I called Arthur to heel and walked over to where I knew Mary and her friend had started. Arthur held himself to the excruciatingly slow pace, although he trembled with anticipation.

Finally, I held his muzzle closed and said, "Sniff." (If I just show him something without holding his mouth closed, he tries to take whatever I'm holding, as retrievers have been bred to do for centuries.)

Arthur snorted on Mary's pink hat, then made a grab for it anyway adding slobber to the dog snot. I wiped the hat on my jeans, pointed to the ground, and braced myself before saying the magic words: "Arthur, track."

And we were off, Arthur dragging me through scratchy brambles; my weight on the leash meant nothing to this eager dog in the prime of life. He overshot where the two tracks parted ways, turned and cast about for perhaps half a second, then yanked me along for another headlong rush weaving between the trees, for what seemed like several miles, but was actually closer to a hundred yards or so.

A sudden shriek of laughter rewarded the questing dog, when Arthur found Mary huddled beneath a shrub. Seeing that she was happy wrestling with Arthur, I dropped the leash and leaned against a tree, trying to catch my breath. There's a saying: If your dog is fat, you don't get enough exercise. But it's perfectly possible for your dog to be in the peak of health, while you're woefully out of shape.

Resolving henceforth to exercise Arthur with long walks instead of by sitting on the porch throwing a tennis ball, I gathered enough breath to thank Mary and return her damp and disheveled hat, then held Arthur's head between my hands and looked deep into the soul shining from his honest brown eyes.

"You. Are. EXcellent," I whispered fiercely, proudly. He had passed what was supposed to be a difficult test, and made it look easy and fun.

Arthur Discovers a Pair of Little Brown Bats

Sunday evening, just at dusk, I was sitting on the front step enjoying the cool breeze. Arthur padded around, inquisitive, snuffling for something interesting. Since some of our local critters (ground bees, skunks, and porcupines) prefer solitude to the unsolicited company of a bumptious eighty-pound retriever who pants and drools, I try to intercede when possible, which means I have to keep an eye on him at all times when we're outside.

So I noticed immediately when he found something that arrested his attention. Ears perked up as far as floppy, golden-furred ears could go, tail wagging fast, Arthur pressed his nose to the ground next to the house wall. Snorting loudly, he then proceeded to start licking at something I couldn't see. Well now, that couldn't be good.

Dogs are notorious for their dietary indiscretion, eating poop being one of their worst vices, and I shudder to admit, Arthur is no exception. This time it seemed he was intent on some mouse droppings.

"Arthur, NO!" I said, appalled. Ugh! And he wonders why when I share a sandwich, I pull pieces off for him instead of letting him take a bite?

Arthur suddenly pretended to find a patch of dandelion utterly enthralling.

Getting up, I went over to the mouse scat, not thrilled to have mice. Sure enough, there was the evidence -- scattered quarter-inch dark-brown droppings that resembled grains of wild rice. But wait a second, how did that one get caught in a spider web?

Even the smallest mouse would have destroyed the silky strands. which meant it must have ... fallen? From above? There was only the wooden board-and-batten slats of the house wall, and the underside of the eave above.

Was it mouse poop? Just maybe ... excited, I told Arthur to sit-stay, and went inside for a flashlight. When I came back out, I slowly shone the beam on the dark crevice where the roof met the wall.

A brown and soft-furred face peered myopically back at me. A bat! Then another face pushed forward! Not just one, but two of these nocturnal insect-eaters were snuggled together, waiting for it to get dark enough to come out and eat mosquitoes.

According to Cornell, one Little Brown Bat (I kid you not; that is the real common name of *myotis lucifugus*) can eat 1,200 bugs in just ONE HOUR. Plus, each mosquito eaten is one less mosquito breeding.

Perhaps I'm biased because I hate stinging, disease-ridden insects, but still, Little Brown Bats are downright cute. They're about half the size of a domestic mouse, with big, dark-brown ears, a nub of a nose, and a mouth that appears to be smiling.

Many mammals can glide (flying squirrels, for instance), but bats are capable of true flight. Despite their appearance, bats are more closely related to humans than to rodents. Also, interestingly, bats that navigate by echolocation (like our Little Brown Bats), can reposition the bone inside their ear to more precisely detect the echo of their cries. Another fun bat fact: because of their hind claws, bats hang upside-down with no effort; in fact, it takes effort to let go.

Many species of bats in the United States are being decimated by White Nose Syndrome, a fungus that is baffling scientists. If colonies continue to decline, we may be in for some serious problems, for both our health and our food crops. It's not just illegal, but ecologically unsound to kill bats. If you get one in the house, it's probably young and stupid, and terrified out of its wits. Instead of screaming and flailing about, and increasing his fear, try just being quiet, turning off the lights and leaving the door or a window open. If he has a chance to calm down, most likely the bat will find his way out.

Of course, if a bat bites a human, the bat should be tested for rabies. If the bat escapes, the person bitten will be prescribed a relatively mild series of five vaccine shots and one or two antibody injections. The painful ordeal of shots in the stomach are thankfully a thing of the past.

Bats are often attracted to small, dark spaces. Many people are unaware of their presence, as I was, or don't mind giving up the millions of mosquitoes these tiny animals eat. For those who do object, the most humane thing to do is to prevent them from setting up residence in the Spring, or offer them something better. Most nature centers, including our own Lime Hollow, offer ready-made bat houses, or kits or plans to build your own, to coax any unwanted House Bats into relocating.

As the evening turned to twilight, I went inside with Arthur, leaving the bats to their nightly feast. I sincerely wished them good health and good hunting.

Can Arthur Resist an Aromatic Pot Roast?

My five-year-old Golden Retriever and I went to my friend Lucille's house to celebrate Christmas. Lucille and I sat on the floor with Arthur, beside the light-up ceramic tree.

There was a box beneath the tree for me, and I grinned to see no less than four merrily-wrapped presents for Arthur. Only four times before this had he been given presents to unwrap, and with a year in between; but it was obvious he remembered what to do.

Tail waving in an arc on the carpet, he madly tore into the first present I handed to him. With his freshly-manicured paws firmly holding the squishy item, he ripped the paper into gleeful shreds, shaking his head with each hunk until the floor was littered with colorful scraps. Finally the brown head and big dark eyes of a teddy bear were available to his teeth, and he pulled the toy from its cocoon of festive wrappings.

Quickly I took it from him, so I could admire it before it was hopelessly drenched in dog drool. It was very soft, very cute, and bless Lucille's heart, entirely without a squeaker.

I find the sound of squeaky toys only slightly less enjoyable than being bitten by a rabid ferret, so Lucille buys Arthur's toys in the baby section to avoid the kitchen-table emergency-surgery squeakectomy that I perform on all squeaky toys.

The other three gifts, to Arthur's delight, were food. One was some sort of canine-healthy popcorn shaped like little dogs (if you have a vivid imagination), but of course I can't show you one now; a bag of what looks like little red checkers is supposedly pepperoni-flavored, smells vaguely like play-doh, and has an enthusiastic paws-up from Arthur (but he also cheerfully eats horse poop, so I don't put much faith in his food reviews); and the third claims to taste like pizza, and smells invitingly of Italian seasoning, but so far I've been able to resist temptation.

By the time we cleared the merry mess away, dinner was done. "Dinner" is an understatement here; Lucille has elevated pot roast to a sublime art form. The scent alone had me euphoric, and I decided I'd rather be able to devote my full attention to the food as it deserved, rather than have any chores lurking in the back of my mind while I ate.

So with Lucille's help, I gathered up the things I wanted to take out to the car. Leaving Arthur in downstay in the living room, Lucille and I bundled up to go outside. As I stood by the door after putting my boots on, I decided, rather grinchlike, to put Arthur to a difficult test.

"Lucille," I asked, "can you put a little roast beef and gravy on a plate, and set it on the living room floor? If Arthur doesn't touch it while we're outside, he can have anything you want to give him. But if he eats it, he can't have anything else." Yeah, I know it sounds mean, but I knew he could do it.

Probably.

Even Lucille, Arthur's staunchest defender, didn't have much faith in his self-control. She did as I asked, but uncharacteristically argued that he would get treats either way. The task was made enormously more challenging by the fact that Arthur watched Lucille set the plate on the floor, not me, and every week she puts a plate of leftovers on the floor for him in exactly this manner.

"Leave it alone," I intoned from out of his sight in the kitchen. "Arthur. Leave. It. ALONE."

Then we went out, shutting the door behind us.

We were gone maybe seven minutes, and I'll spare you the suspense: he never touched it. Tensely he lay across the room from the plate, holding himself in check by sheer will alone.

Wordlessly I strode to his side, stood for a moment watching his tail thump in anticipation, then suddenly bent and ruffled his fur. "Excellent! Good puppy!" (No matter how old a dog actually is, when he does well, he's a "good puppy," and when he misbehaves, he instantly ages to "bad dog.")

Recognizing an invitation when one is given, Arthur cleared the distance between himself and the plate in one bound, practically inhaling the delicious meat.

For the rest of our visit, I tried not to notice how much Lucille fed him. (She knows to not give him fatty scraps or a lot of gravy, so he was in no danger.) To my surprise and relief, he still fit through the door on our way out.

Unfortunately, Arthur's favorite toy is whichever is newest. After a few hours of even the gentlest mouthing by a happy, eighty-pound retriever, his Christmas teddy bear wasn't nearly as cuddly with a gummy punk-rock spike hairdo.

Arthur's Exciting Car Ride

Last night I had to move my car from the front of the driveway to the back, so I invited my Golden Retriever along. "Arthur, want to go for a ride in the car?"

Like most dogs, Arthur loves the car, and this surprise invitation had him dancing with joy, quite literally, stepping on my toes with his eighty pounds of excitement.

"You're on my foot, you big ox," I said mildly, more amused by his enthusiasm than actually injured. But by the time I said it, he was already at the door, panting with anticipation.

I opened the door wide and hesitated in the doorway -- a test. Despite his adrenaline, Arthur held himself to a standstill beside me, impatiently but politely waiting for me to cross the threshold first.

"Excellent," I whispered to him, stepping down as I thumped his furry side.

Out he shot as if from a cannon, clearing the stoop entirely in his eagerness to get to the car, so he could stand beside it and wait for me. His gold brushy tail swished back and forth so hard I could feel the breeze of it from a few feet away in the still night air.

I eyed his muddy feet with a rueful shake of my head. When I first got this new-to-me car, I vowed to keep it as clean as humanly possible. The operative word there is "humanly." Oh, there's a nice big blanket spread out over the entire backseat, but unless the front passenger seat is occupied, that's where he ends up. At least most of the mud comes off on the blanket, which is easier to clean than the upholstery.

After letting him in the back and shutting the door, I climbed in and started the motor. Arthur jumped neatly into the shotgun seat, and panted happily. I tried not to look at his feet on the tan cloth seat.

Arthur was looking forward, expecting me to drive out onto the street, but I just twisted to see behind me and backed up about twenty feet, then switched off the motor and turned to Arthur.

"We're home!" I announced, as if we'd returned after a fifteen-mile trip to town instead of a short amble down our own driveway.

Dogs are pretty easy to please. Arthur was every bit as excited to return as he'd been to leave. Then I offered him something even more exciting.

"Arthur, want to help me feed birds?"

I'm not certain he understands every word I say, but he sure knows the word "help." To him it means he gets to spend time with me, do something, and get praised for it -- all on top of the car ride!

Scooping some sunflower seed into a coffee can, I handed Arthur his toothmarked empty plastic jug, and we set out by flashlight behind the house to the feeder. Arthur's milk jug had no real purpose, except to make him feel useful, but of course I'd never tell him that.

We turned the corner behind the house, and I just caught a brief glimpse of a small silvery-gray furry shape gracefully leaping off the birdfeeder into the old pines above. A flying squirrel! Here in central New York!

"Arthur, stay," I said quietly, and walked the rest of the way to the feeder alone, moving slowly so as not to alarm the adorable creature who was probably not far away. Quietly I dumped the seed into the feeder and motioned Arthur to accompany me back to the house.

Flying squirrels don't really fly, but they can glide using the furred membrane that stretches from wrist to ankle. The smallest squirrel, they are also our only nocturnal squirrel, and their huge dark eyes will melt your heart. They prefer old pine snags for nesting, and if they successfully avoid owls, weasels and housecats, can live to be five or six years old.

Unfortunately, in my rush to look up flying squirrels, I forgot to take the empty milk jug from Arthur. He never chews on toys or items he purloins (which is why I still have a camera, cell phone and wallet) so I didn't even notice he'd brought it into the house with him.

Not, that is, until about three AM, when my beloved insomniac dog decided to play a game of solitaire fetch with the thing by throwing it across the hardwood floor and then pouncing on it, creating an incredible racket. Half-asleep, I stumbled out of bed to exchange a small fuzzy football for the noisy milk jug, then went back to bed while he continued to amuse himself more quietly.

Arthur Visits the Post Office

This past Saturday morning was way too gorgeous for me to refuse my Golden Retriever's eager entreaty to accompany me on a walk down the street to pick up the mail. What most people regard as a routine stop or even a tedious chore, Arthur considers a delightful Adventure, with a capital A.

I peered outside. The lack of snow and recent warm temperatures had turned the yard into a morass. If I tried to run some of the excited energy out of this eighty-pound fuzzball with a frisbee, he'd be a muddy mess, unfit to be seen in public. Reluctantly opting for beauty over intelligence, I clipped the unnecessary but legally-required leash to his collar, then I pulled my coat on and stepped out into the unseasonable sunshine, with Arthur at heel.

Oh, how he wanted to run and sniff and frolic, and maybe find something to bring to me! But his impeccable breeding made him choose my approval over his own fun, and he held himself with an effort to my human pace, which must seem ridiculously slow to him.

When we arrived at the quaint little local Post Office with its window flowerbox, there were a fair number of people going in an out. Arthur and I made friends while we went in and waited for the crowd to thin enough for us to get to the boxes. One older gentleman petted Arthur and laughed, which of course made Arthur delirious with joy. His brushy gold tail wagged hard against his sides, and he panted with excitement. Although he shoves his way jealously between me and any other dog I might decide to pet, Arthur sees nothing wrong with him being petted by other humans.

I love showing off my beautiful, brilliant chum, so I bragged that he could derive square roots, which of course led to a demonstration. First I cautioned our audience to keep the answers below ten -- not because Arthur can't count any higher, but because more than ten of his thunderous deep woofs is deafening. I told Arthur to sit-stay, then walked the length of the six-foot leash away, to stand with my hands behind my back.

Inviting math questions, I asked Arthur for the answers, and he wowed the small gathering with the correct number of barks, which he followed by running to jump up on me. Like most dogs, Arthur loves jumping up, especially if his paws are muddy and I'm wearing a clean coat. Getting praised for jumping up is his reward for paying close enough attention to get the math right.

Eventually we reemerged from the Post Office, with several letters and one of those free weekly newspapers. When I tapped him on top of the head with the newspaper, he gleefully snatched it and declared it his. Proudly he held his head up, a Golden Retriever doing what Golden Retrievers have been bred to do for generations. There is nothing Arthur loves to do quite as much as carrying something around.

Arthur happily carried the newspaper all the way back home, throwing his head occasionally, wagging constantly. What a terrific outing! It's easy to show a dog a good time.

Once we got home I discovered that walking a dog on wet roads is pretty much just as bad as running him on muddy turf. Arthur's legs, feet and belly were no longer gold and silky, but mud-brown and stringy. I had to get a jug of warm water from the sink, sluice him off and towel him dry before he was fit to come in. He held onto the newspaper through it all, only giving it up when we went inside and I rummaged in the biscuit box to give him a well-deserved reward. What a good puppy.

Memorial Day Fireworks

Sunday evening we were just sitting around quietly minding our own business, when all of a sudden my Golden Retriever woofed under his breath. Arthur is breathtakingly beautiful when he's alert, with his eyes bright, fuzzy golden ears perked up, and every line of his noble body held in a state of readiness. He woofed again, louder, but still as if uncertain. I got up to check it out, as I always do. I'd feel really stupid if I ignored the dog's warning and found out later that there really was someone breaking into my car or something.

Arthur tagged along as I went to the front porch and looked out. His job is to raise the alarm, and my job as alpha is to keep the pack safe. He appreciates that I take him seriously, even though he occasionally "warns" me of such potential threats as the cat in the next room mumbling in his sleep, or a bluejay scolding a crow across the road and down two doors.

But Sunday was a bona fide unusual occurrence: the neighbors were setting off fireworks. Thoroughbred that he is, Arthur shows no fear of the sharp, ear-splitting sounds, but many dogs do, and although he doesn't whine or yelp, I'm sure it hurts his ultra-sensitive ears.

With the Fourth of July celebrations coming up, it's worthwhile to note that when you have a crowd of visitors, lots of food, children, plus general excitement and chaos, there's already lots of potential for problems with the family dog. Add fireworks and you could have a disaster.

Unfortunately, it's all too common for a dog to get lost during a fireworks display. Many dogs will bolt, trying to get away from the terrifying sound, and when exhaustion finally brings them to a halt, they have no idea where they are or how to get home. With everything else going on, it might be hours before the owner even notices the dog is gone, and sets out on a belated search.

It costs nothing to keep your chum safe in a spare room for the duration of the festivities, and could save you much time and worry and perhaps heartache later. If Fido is crate-trained, that's even better, as it provides a quiet, comforting cave for him to retreat to, and you won't have to worry about him gnawing on a table leg in his anxiety. Check on him periodically, to make sure he hasn't dumped his water and to reassure him with your own calm demeanor.

(Cuddling a scared dog won't necessarily convince him there's something to be afraid of, but if you instead act like everything is fine, your dog should take his cue from your relaxed state and assume that if the pack leader is unconcerned, then there is nothing to worry about.)

You don't want your dog milling around with a houseful of guests anyway, particularly if there are unsupervised children present. It's never a good idea to let dogs and kids interact without an adult paying close attention. If the dog is big, no matter how docile he might be, the kid could get stepped on or pawed or knocked over accidentally, and if the dog is small, then he might be the one to be hurt. Prevention is just so much easier.

Even if you don't have any guests for the upcoming holiday, it's still imperative to keep your dog indoors and either with you or someplace you know he will be safe. A snack can often make a difficult time happier for a dog, but if you're giving him something other than dog treats, choose wisely.

There are plenty of healthy scraps from your own meal. Bread is a favorite, and believe it or not, most dogs love vegetables, especially carrots cooked in the beef broth, and nearly anything he sees you scrape off your own plate. Avoid fatty foods, chocolate, and onions or garlic.

After I investigated the peculiar sounds and came back in mildly annoyed instead of alarmed, Arthur padded over to the box of dog biscuits as if showing me where they were. Apparently he thinks I might forget where they're kept, even though they've been in the same place for years.

I handed him three of the miniature snacks one by one, then kissed his big blocky head. Recognizing this gentle dismissal, he laid down and went to sleep with a deep sigh, while the fireworks continued to annoy me for the next hour and a half.

Arthur and the Catbird

Ah, July: time to go hunting wild black raspberries, eaten fresh off the prickly canes, still warm from the sun, their purple juice staining your fingers -- and your dog.

Sometimes I really see the advantages to having a black dog. Sure, they're almost impossible to photograph, but they don't get grass stains on their shoulders when they roll on the fresh-mown lawn, or get purple smears on their face when they shove their nose into your hands while you're holding a handful of ripe berries -- or at least it doesn't show.

Anyone who has a golden retriever is only too familiar with this brazen demand for attention. It's not a hint, it's an anvil, and can result in spilled drinks, dropped items, or even inadvertent purchases on eBay if you happen to be online when he decides that you've ignored him too long.

My cat Sly accompanied us as we foraged along the hedgerow, lagging a few paces behind. "Mrrrooww," he mumbled in felinese.

Wait a second. Sly was behind us, but that meow had definitely come from the shrubs in front of us. Arthur padded ahead, looking for the new friend he could hear but not see. He came to a halt by a small tree, looking up with his signature good-natured curiosity.

The meow we had heard was repeated, coming from a slender gray bird about the size of a bluejay, sporting a bit of black on his head, with rust-red feathers beneath his tail. It was a catbird, one of the few wild creatures to benefit from human development.

According to Cornell, our common Gray Catbird prefers to live in thick patches of shrubs and small trees, like those created by roads, farmland, and suburban housing. Their food is plentiful where humans live: ants, beetles, caterpillars and moths, plus fruit in season. The biggest danger posed by human encroachment is cars, because roadside trees are a favorite habitat, and catbirds tend to fly low.

Some nifty catbird facts: Like their mockingbird relatives, catbirds will readily mimic other birds and animals, even whistles and machinery noises, creating a song which can last for ten minutes. Catbirds winter along the southeastern coast and down into Central America, and both sexes will defend winter territory -- highly unusual in the bird world. The oldest documented catbird was seventeen years old. To entice catbirds into your yard, plant shrubs and fruit trees.

Our catbird chaperone flapped and hopped through the branches of the trees, keeping just ahead of us, periodically mewing more convincingly catlike than

Sly himself. (Fat and indolent, Sly ignored the feathered imposter with disdain.)

I ignored the catbird, too, gathering up as many black raspberries as were ripe, eating some but keeping the best to take home and share with Lynda and Aloysius. In my concentration on finding ripe berries, which can induce a zenlike state of meditation where nothing else exists, I also ignored Arthur, which I usually regret.

My beautiful, beloved chum is a master of disastrous timing with his snout-shoves, and sure enough, he waited till I had I brimming handful of delicious, fragile berries filled with indelible juice before sneaking up on me and suddenly thrusting his big blocky head into my hand, with all the energy and force that a joyful, eighty-pound dog can muster.

"Arthur, no!" I managed to say, way too late to save even one berry. The few that weren't smooshed to purple pulp between my hand and Arthur's furry skull had gone flying in all directions. My hand was now a nice deep purple, and Arthur had half a purple mask and one purple ear.

I wanted to laugh and yell at him at the same time. Instead I hunkered down in the foot-high weeds, trying without much hope to salvage even just one or two luscious berries. Nope, no luck.

On the up side, the squished berries didn't go to waste. Arthur cheerfully licked my hands and then dropped to the ground and wiped at his face with both forepaws. If this was an effort to clean himself, it was a dismal failure. All he did was add a grass stain to the freakish purple stripe down one ear, making him look like a rebellious teenager.

As I watched him lick the last of the berry juice from his jowls, I had to wonder if he hadn't deliberately plotted the whole thing, taking advantage of my inattention to obtain an impromptu snack.

No, no, of course not …

Canine Burglar Alarm Beats Modern Technology Any Day -- Or Night

Sherlock Holmes solved a murder mystery partly because of the "curious incident of the dog in the night-time." The dog in question did nothing in the night, while someone stole a horse from the barn the dog was sleeping in. That, of course, was the curious incident.

Why do dogs bark? One of the commonest traits across the myriad canine breeds, barking is a dog's way of alerting his packmates of danger. While we no longer sleep in caves (well, most of us don't), dogs have continued to warn us when anything is amiss, down through the centuries and despite our frequent disapproval.

Today, most people would prefer their dog not bark at every unusual sound or scent -- but for heaven's sake, if your dog suddenly starts barking in the middle of the night, go investigate. Don't join the ranks of those who ignored their chum's warning and regretted it.

One guy I know of yelled at his dog for barking in the wee hours, and when the "dumb animal" wouldn't quiet down, he actually locked the dog in the bathroom. The guy went downstairs the next morning to discover he'd been robbed. I bet that burglar is still chuckling.

The one thing most likely to deter a burglar isn't a fancy high-tech alarm system; nope, it's a dog. And it doesn't even have to be a big dog -- in fact, the small, yappy ones that dance just out of reach are among the most effective, because the criminal can't get close enough to shut them up and keep them from rousing the entire household.

Nobody gets a Golden Retriever as a guard dog, but your gentle companion might surprise you. Arthur's grandfather once leaped out the window of the parked truck where he'd been left, to stand growling between his owner Pam and an unknown, unkempt man who skulked across the dark parking lot to confront her. Pam was scared speechless, but no words were needed; the man fled at the sight of an eighty-pound dog with teeth bared. Tigger may have saved Pam's life that night -- an internationally-titled champion show dog who had never before shown the slightest sign of aggression, and never did again. Such is Arthur's heritage.

Once advantage of a purebred dog acquired from a reputable breeder is that you know your pup's lineage. In many cases, you can meet the parents and form a reasonable expectation of your dog's future temperament and tendencies. Health problems are kept to a minimum by conscientious, responsible breeders, and any undesirable traits are bred out of the line.

But there are also many thoroughly lovable, loving doggy chums available at the local shelters, dogs whose backgrounds can be more or less deduced from their present physique or habits, and who are often highly appreciative when given the things most purebreds take for granted: a home, food, a kind word, a gentle touch.

The mature dogs know what it's like to be hungry, cold, unwanted, and alone, and they value a good home. Frequently, these dogs are also highly intelligent; they've had to be, just to survive.

The canine celebrity Benji was rescued from a shelter. In those movies, Benji did all his own tricks, because unlike purebreds like Lassie, there were no look-alikes, each with their own specialized training.

You want the ultimate in unique "designer" dogs? The shelter has a variety of sizes, looks, and personalities to choose from.Create your own impressive-sounding breed name and tell folks he's worth over a thousand dollars (which will be true, when you fall in love with him) and if some night he barks and you heed his warning, he may well prove himself priceless by saving you and your family.

In addition to Arthur's playful bark when he answers math questions, he also has a deeper, serious-sounding WOOF that means "someone's coming" -- either that, or "some sort of critter is in the yard." Regardless of the hour, I always check it out. Lately I've startled a fox, three deer, and several opossums (or maybe the same one several times) with my flashlight.

One of the most peaceful, beneficial wild animals we have in this area is the Virginia Opossum: shy, nocturnal creatures who eat mice, rats, all sorts of grubs and bugs, and even rattlesnakes (adult opossums are immune to snake venom.) And unlike other, perhaps cuter, animals with better public relations (raccoons, skunks, and foxes), opossums are highly resistant to the rabies virus.

In the spring, opossums wander about looking for love; unfortunately, many of these charming marsupials aren't paying sufficient attention to much else. While I'm not suggesting that anyone behind the wheel risk their life trying to avoid an animal, still, opossums rarely dart out in front of a car. Generally they're meandering slowly, with their famous hip-swing (their skeleton is arranged a little differently than ours, and the hip joint gives them this peculiar gait.) They're ambling along in the dark, minding their own business, when an oncoming car's headlights suddenly blind them, and they freeze with fear.

If you can safely slow down or steer around them, you'll have the satisfaction of knowing that you've spared the life of a harmless individual who values his life every bit as much as we value ours. And who knows? That opossum or one of his cousins may someday repay your kindness by catching and eating a rattlesnake in your child's backyard.

Arthur Enjoys the Annual Golden Retriever Reunion in Little York

Friday afternoon I gave Arthur a thorough bath on the lawn. Like most golden retrievers, he loves attention of any kind, plus he loves water. In addition, he's been taught the show-ring "stand-and-stay" command (this is handy any time you want your dog to stand still, including at the vet's.) This combination makes him one of the easiest dogs to bathe.

The closest Arthur comes to misbehaving is when he tries to drink from the hose as I'm rinsing him off. Afterward, I rubbed him partially dry with a towel, worked in some of my salon conditioner, and finished drying him off with a tennis ball.

Playing fetch on a sunny day with a slight breeze is one of the easiest ways to turn a wet, energetic idiot into a huggably dry, mellow companion. Arthur's tail always dries first, even though that's the longest fur on his body. By the time the rest of him was dry, Arthur was calm enough to lay quietly while I trimmed his foot-fur down like a show dog, and brushed him to a fluffy burnished gold. The evening sun shone with brilliant luster on his soft and silky coat, and I deemed him presentable.

"Arthur, OK," I released him from stand-stay.

Hungry now that he'd expended his pent-up energy, Arthur padded sedately over to sprinkle the rosebushes (it's a Mystery why they don't bloom), paying no attention to the hummingbirds directly above, as they swooped and chittered at each other with their namesake humming sound.

Confident in their own speed and aerial agility, hummingbirds amply reward the minimal effort it takes to maintain a nectar feeder. These tiny, brilliantly-colored birds provide spectacular entertainment as they zip about, hover and bicker amongst themselves -- all within feet or sometimes inches of their human benefactors. Indeed, the popularity of feeding these feathered jewels has actually encouraged them to gradually push the northern edge of their range, showing up now as far north as Saskatchewan.

In addition to flower nectar and tree sap, hummingbirds also consume large numbers of tiny insects, found in flowers or gleaned from tree bark, or even taken on the wing.

Ruby-throated hummingbirds are the only one commonly found in the northeast United States. The male is unmistakable with his jewel-like ruby-colored gorget (birder-speak for the area beneath the chin), but both genders have the distinctive metallic green back.

The female builds a nest of bits of leaves and spider silk, then looks around for a mate. After laying her eggs, she then raises the young on her own. Hatching out naked and blind, the babies are able to leave the nest after less than a month.

Most ruby-throated hummingbirds spend the winter in Central America, returning to New York around the end of April. Come fall, they build up fat reserves right before setting out on their long journey, so it's important to keep their feeder full for at least a week after the last hummingbird is seen. (It's a myth that leaving the feeder up will interfere with their instinct to migrate.) My yard always seems a bit forlorn when the last of these colorful personalities leaves.

Arthur got a full grooming Friday because Saturday was the annual Golden Reunion: a fun day for golden retrievers put together by the Golden Retriever Rescue of Central New York. People from all over bring their goldens to compete in friendly challenges, check out breed-specific merchandise, buy raffle tickets, and swap stories with other owners.

At ten in the morning, Arthur smelled like my floral-scented shampoo; by eleven AM, he and most of the other eighty goldens smelled strikingly of dead snails, courtesy of the nearby lake. Fortunately, the humans were all self-selected dog people, so nobody minded.

The first event was the Egg Carry. More than a dozen eager goldens lined up on the side of the paved basketball court, and at the signal, each owner gave their dog a raw egg to carry in his or her mouth to the other side. Arthur was one of only four goldens who made it to the other side with their egg intact. We four then had to go the length of the basketball court to determine a winner; Arthur and another gold soul tied for first place. I was so proud of my clever chum!

The next event consisted of three hula hoops laid out in a line on the pavement. Walking beside his owner, each dog had to sit inside the first hoop, go sit in the second, then lay down in the third, returning by sitting in the first two hoops again -- absurdly simple for a dog like Arthur, who walks everywhere at heel.

When it came our turn, however, Arthur refused to step inside the hoop. He dithered around it, pressed up against me to avoid it, even leaped over it, as everyone laughed. Dismayed and mystified (I still don't know why he reacted like that), after the event was over and the judge started picking up the hoops, I asked if we could play with them. Understanding, she just told me where to leave them when we were through.

Armed with a pocket full of liver treats, I told Arthur to sit-stay while I scattered all twenty or so hoops around him. Under the influence of verbal encouragement and blatant bribery, Arthur tentatively stepped in the hoops, discovered that they didn't bite him (or whatever it was that he expected them to do), and quickly decided to ignore them in favor of the food. Within fifteen minutes he approached a row of ten hoops, and deftly sat in each in turn.

The other goldens had better watch out for him next year!

Arthur Visits the "Grand Canyon of Pennsylvania"

This weekend, I took my golden retriever further afield than he's ever been, all the way to the Leonard Harrison State Park near Wellsboro, Pennyslvania. The park we proposed to visit boasts miles of trails, some steep enough to make a goat think twice. I invited Arthur along for the two-hour drive.

Situated on the East Rim of the "Grand Canyon of Pennsylvania," this beautiful park offers breathtaking views from two different trails, the Overlook and Turkey Path. The first consists of half a mile of moderate incline; the latter descends 800 vertical feet to the stream at the bottom of the wooded canyon, with switchbacks and even several sets of stairs, whose difficulties of construction I shuddered to contemplate.

For the most part Arthur slept during the ride. He's never been the type to hang his head out an open car window (a dangerous habit, as road debris thrown up by car tires can injure your dog, or even blind him), so we had the luxury of fresh air (except for that section of highway where some unlucky soul ran over a skunk.)

Once at the park, I put the requisite leash on Arthur and affixed his backpack, which held water for us both, a plastic bag in case of emergency, a small bag of biscuits for him, and two apples for me. An eighty-pound retriever in the prime of life, Arthur loves the backpack, as it invariably means he's about to enjoy a lengthy walk with his human, every dog's favorite activity.

We chose the Overlook trail first, as a sort of warm-up. Delirious at the prospect of adventure, Arthur wagged at everyone we met, while I kept him under strict command, forcing him to sit and allow people to pet him in a pseudo-civilized manner, all too aware of the steep incline only a few feet away.

The trail led through the woods to a lookout point, where a wooden deck offers views straight down to the creek as well as out across the chasm. After a few minutes spotting and identifying some vultures overhead, we walked back up, the gentle incline a small, easily-overlooked warning of the tortuous trek to come.

After giving Arthur a drink by filling my hands at the water fountain (he would've cheerfully schlurped straight from the spigot, but oddly enough, some people object to this practice) and giving him a chance to leave his signature on a discreet section of local flora, we turned toward Turkey Path, and began our descent.

For most four-legged creatures, going down a set of stairs is much more difficult than going up, and Arthur isn't the most graceful of canines, but he did it, remaining at my side except where the trail grew too narrow. Down, down we went, until finally the path levelled off and we arrived at Pine Creek, the deceptively small stream that singlehandedly carved this thirty-seven-mile-long marvel from the living earth.

I was happy to reach this halfway point (geographically speaking), but Arthur was absolutely ecstatic. Like most retrievers, he loves water, and knows from experience that on outings like this I'm pretty lenient. He gazed longingly at the water in eloquent silence, and I relented.

"Okay," I said softly.

The first syllable was barely out before Arthur splashed with abandon into midstream, where he stood belly-deep to lap his fill. Then, with a silly grin on his furry face, he looked me in the eye and laid down.

"Arthur!" I yelled, exasperated, gaining the attention of the dozen or so folks in the immediate area. "Come," I hissed through clenched teeth (it's hard to hiss the word "come," but I managed.)

Meekly Arthur stood and waded back, the water falling from his coat in sheets. A foot in front of me, he stopped and shook vigorously. Great, now we were both soaked.

The arduous trek back up was a far different experience than what I now realized was an absurdly easy trip down. This was one of the rare times I actually encouraged Arthur to walk ahead of me and pull on the leash, giving me a boost. Exhausted, I made it to the summit eventually, gasping for breath.

Topside, Arthur padded along, unconcerned about the thoroughly disreputable state of his coat brought about by walking around sopping wet on dusty trails. I had forgotten to bring along a towel, but after half an hour I pronounced him fit to get in the car. Honestly, I wasn't much better off, sartorially speaking, than my dog.

Hiking tip: Always park at the BOTTOM of the hill.

The Terrible Truth Behind Squeaky Toys

We spend a lot of money on our pets, but few of them get to accompany us outside the home or car. Most dogs would be delighted to go anywhere with their human packmates, even to places we find dull and uninteresting, such as the bank or the office-supply store. Arthur considers a trip to the mall the highlight of his day, even though I make him stay out in the hall while I'm in stores.

While well-behaved dogs are allowed in places like the Carousel Mall (if sometimes grudgingly), there are laws prohibiting animals where food is served, despite the fact that Arthur is cleaner than many of the people I've seen in the grocery store.

The biggest determining factor is the phrase "well-behaved." There are several training requirements that shop owners can reasonably ask of any dog brought into their store: first, that he be reliably housetrained. Second, no canine kleptomaniacs. Third, and most important, that your dog pose no danger to anyone else in the store, human or otherwise. Many pet shops welcome dogs on a leash -- but please remember, a leash may not be enough to prevent your dog from suddenly grabbing a pet on display for sale, and even just barking might be enough to frighten small animals or birds to death. If there's a sign in a pet store requesting no dogs beyond a certain point, it's because some of the critters kept there, like bunnies and chinchillas, are so susceptible to stress that the mere sight of a predator may panic them into hurting themselves in an attempt to get away, or even give them a heart attack on the spot.

Most dogs have an innate instinct to attack prey-type animals. Pet toy makers have long capitalized on the average dog's atavistic enjoyment of killing small animals; this is the underlying concept behind "squeaky toys." The dog bites down on these small, often furry toys and the toy emits a shriek of agony. Good boy, Fido. And then folks are taken completely by surprise when Fido kills the escaped pet hamster.

None of Arthur's toys squeak, for exactly that reason. They are either purchased squeakless, or rendered so by an emergency squeakectomy with my jackknife. (A tiny hole in the squeaker is sufficient to silence the thing.)

Doing this has the added attraction that the dog can't lay there and repeatedly squeak the toy over and over until you're ready to scream yourself.

The ability of a dog to suppress the instinct to kill is amazing, and it's a very worthwhile trait to train. Some breeds are already inclined to live peaceably with what their wolf ancestors would have viewed as a tasty snack.

Heaven knows Arthur has had ample opportunity to supplement his diet with cat and other assorted animal entreés. yet his desire to please me is more important; and Arthur's uncle Hobbes even refrained from harming a baby red fox who snuggled up against him (a lengthy story already told elsewhere.)

Red fox are a common canid in rural areas, even denning and raising kits in surprising proximity to man. Last summer, I was startled to see four young foxes cavorting in a field not far from the paved road. While capable of digging their own burrows, red fox are not above taking over a groundhog den, as was the case here.

For over a week I smiled to see them there on my way home in the twilight, and often stopped to enjoy this rare glimpse into the lives of these usually timid creatures. A neighbor even set up a tripod for his video camera to preserve the drama of the mother fox bringing home a rabbit for dinner.

Although classified under the broad division of Canidae, foxes are not in the Canis family with dogs and wolves. Their eyes more closely resemble a cat's than a dog's, with vertical slit pupils. While not as agile in trees as the gray fox, red fox are accomplished climbers in their constant quest for food. True omnivores, foxes will eat almost anything, including insects, carrion, rodents, snakes, berries, apples, wild grapes, and cherries.

Because they are lone hunters, as opposed to hunting in packs, foxes are unlikely to take down prey larger than themselves, and their size is deceptive: an adult red fox weighs an average of just twelve to fifteen pounds, about as much as a housecat. Most of their apparent size is merely fur, which can be four inches thick in the winter. In summer coat, a red fox looks rather like a long-legged weasel, after all that glorious winter pelage sheds out. (A fox in spring or early summer with clumps of scraggly fur falling off is probably perfectly healthy, only shedding. Still, it's always best to enjoy wildlife from a distance; rabies has no visible physical signs, only erratic behavioral symptoms.)

Red fox also indulge in an astonishing repertoire of vocalizations. They can bark and whine, but will also spit and chuff like a cat when annoyed, yodel in greeting to loved ones, and when lonely they can scream like a woman. One night while sitting on a friend's porch, we watched a neighbor leisurely jogging -- until a fox scream rent the evening, and the jogger started sprinting.

Arthur has never met a fox, but I hope if he ever does, he'll be as much of a gentleman as Hobby was.

Arthur Enjoys the Jim Schug Trail at Dryden Lake

Sunday was so unexpectedly beautiful for the penultimate day of November, that I simply couldn't justify staying in my pajamas much past noon. Only a few miles away was Dryden Lake, with a beautiful and well-kept trail which we had yet to explore. So I threw on a light coat, grabbed the leash, and invited my Golden Retriever to jump into the car.

Not surprisingly, we weren't the only ones to think of this idea; several different dogs were being treated to this last glorious glimpse of autumn sunshine. A cute little spaniel trotted alongside one couple, a beagle led a woman who wore a bright blue scarf, and Joey, a friend from Lime Hollow, had his black-and-white Boston Terrier puppy out under the blue sky, happily rustling their way through the fallen leaves.

A quiet stream runs beside the path, and on our way past the trestle bridge the sound of water falling on water made me curious, so we turned off the trail and made our way, me and my eager dog, down a rather muddy bank. The sound came from a small rivulet escaping a well-tended beaver dam, bristling with fresh tree limbs and mud. A heap of newly-cut branches lay piled not far away, the ends gnawed to points bearing the signature imprint of chisel teeth, some sporting bare patches where the bark had been stripped away for a meal. Unfortunately, at that time of day the dam-builders were most likely snoozing in their lodge, so we didn't get to see them.

However, in the small marshy area to the left of the trail we saw a row of several ducks standing at attention on a waterlogged pine amid the dead trees, and at the other end of the path, a sharp nibbling sound pinpointed a red squirrel sitting calmly not three feet up from the ground and barely five feet off the trail, where my eighty-pound retriever stood panting in his direction. Perhaps the squirrel is used to dogs on a leash, or maybe he was just intent on his acorn. Either way, he was adorable, and I regretted not bringing my camera.

Arthur considers every stranger a potential source of attention and petting; the proximity of those going in the opposite direction on this fairly narrow trail proved a challenge to my canine Affection Sponge. With heroic self-restraint, he maintained his sedate "heel" position, only once whipping his head around as we passed too close to an older couple, begging a quick pat from the nice lady, who laid her hand on his head as if in a brief benediction and smiled down at him, making his tail wag so hard it hit his ribs.

Unfortunately, it gets dark in mid-afternoon at this time of year, so we had to leave long before we had hiked even a fraction of the path, but it'll be there when we go back.

For a five-year-old Golden Retriever, of course, our four-mile hike on a flat, manicured path was barely a warmup, a tease rather than a workout. When I lifted him down out of the car, he took off in crazy circles around the yard. I let him run out of steam while I leaned against the car. (Throwing a frisbee until your dog is exhausted every evening is great exercise for the dog, but doesn't do much for your own cardiovascular health.)

Only when Arthur had romped enough to notice that he was thirsty did we troop inside, where I refilled the water dish twice, and then gave him his dinner, garnishing the dry kibble with tiny, luscious bits of lean pan-fried steak.

Local Gray Squirrels Entertain Arthur while Caching Peanuts for Winter

My Golden Retriever loves to carry stuff, which will come as no surprise to anyone who lives with a retriever. Since it's easier to give him something I don't mind getting all slobbery instead of letting him decide what to grab, I usually hand him a bag of peanuts as we head outside in the evening. It's light, waterproof, and if he spills some there's no need to clean up; they'll magically disappear within the hour.

In addition to several birdfeeders and birdbaths, I have a bird-proof squirrel feeder. Yes, you read that right, this is a clear-fronted wooden box with a hinged lid. The first bushytail to encounter this puzzle took about three seconds to figure it out, but it successfully prevents the bluejays from stealing and hiding the peanuts as fast as they can fly off with them. The frustrated jays occasionally harry a squirrel if they see one carrying a peanut, and sometimes even pester the fuzzy rodent into dropping his snack, but they don't get much in the way of positive reinforcement. Plus, either they don't particularly like sunflower seeds, or they have difficulty perching on the birdfeeders, because we don't have many of these noisy birds hanging about.

Once we got to the squirrel feeder, I asked for the (now slimy) bag of peanuts, which Arthur cheerfully dropped into my open hand.

The easiest way I've found to get a dog to drop something you want is to offer him something better. If he's holding a toy and you say "drop" while offering a treat in the palm of your hand, chances are he can't spit that toy out fast enough. Soon all you have to do is say "drop" or even just hold out your hand, and he will immediately surrender whatever he's carrying. (Trying to pry a dog's jaws apart with your hands just makes him clench harder, and attempting to pull it away from him is, to the dog, nothing more than a fun game of tuggie.)

Without the bag to carry, Arthur sniffed around the big tree the squirrel feeder is on. He can read the myriad scent-trails of various rodents as easily as we read a newspaper, and he spent the time it took me to clean out and fill up the feeder inhaling, sneezing, and standing tippytoes on his back feet, stretching up the trunk with his nose reaching past my five-foot height to catch every last bit of the fascinating rodential odor.

The squirrels themselves aren't really afraid of my fuzzy gold dog, and only retreat as far as absolutely necessary, perching on a branch a foot above his farthest reach, lashing their bottle-brush tails and taunting him in Squirrelese. They have much to do before the snow comes, and Arthur is delaying them.

Several interesting gray squirrel fun facts: they can be gray, white, black, brown or anything in between, the odder colors more likely in suburban areas where it's not as important to be camouflage-gray. They don't hibernate, and don't hoard a large amount of food in one secure location as chipmunks do. Instead they bury thousands of individual items, remembering the locations accurately enough to find them months later through snow. Gray squirrels have also been observed pretending to bury a tidbit, complete with the final pat-down of dirt, while continuing to hold the item in their mouth, if they think they're being watched.

Gray squirrels live an average of twelve years in the wild, and as long as twenty in captivity. They are one of the few mammals which can descend a tree headfirst, because their hind feet rotate so they can use the claws both going up and down. For those who play Scrabble, the nest of sticks and leaves that squirrels build in the fork of a tree is technically referred to as a "drey."

The genus name *Sciurus* is derived from Greek for "tail-shadow," referring to their habit of sitting in the shade of their own tail.

For me, the point to putting up a squirrel feeder is to keep the squirrels out of the birdfeeders. As far as that goes, it's a resounding success: the squirrels eat from their feeder and the birds from the birdfeeders as if the Seed Police were watching. The only place where birds and squirrels overlap is the birdbath -- which is a misnomer, as more birds drink from the thing than actually bathe in it, and squirrels and even chipmunks drink from from it as well.

The only trouble is, peanuts aren't cheap, so it costs about eight dollars a week in peanuts to safeguard five dollars' worth of sunflower seeds. Oh well, at least it gives Arthur some harmless canine entertainment.

How to Trick Your Dog into Letting Go of a Dead Mole

Arthur padded up to me on the porch, and he wasn't panting. After racing around the yard, he always pants, even in negative temperatures; either something was drastically wrong with him, or he had something in his mouth.

Since Arthur was acting normally, and a good-sized Golden can conceal a tennis ball with those floppy lips, I held out my hand and said, "Arthur. Drop it."

Wagging hard, Arthur spit out a small, sodden item into my hand. It took a moment for me to recognize it: a mole, one of Nature's most efficient excavation experts. It was very dead. We'd only been outside for about an hour, so it definitely hadn't been alive when he found it.

Eastern moles are not rodents; they're members of the same family as shrews, distantly related to anteaters. About the size of a chipmunk, they have incredibly soft, velvety fur that repels dirt and lacks the natural "nap" of most furry critters -- it can bend either forward or back, to facilitate moving about in the confines of a tunnel. Also, their blood has almost twice the amount of hemoglobin (the part that carries oxygen) that ours does, a handy adaptation for someone who rarely breathes fresh air.

Living most of their lives underground, their eyes barely discern light and dark, and not much else. To make up for this, their sense of hearing is exceptionally keen, although they don't have external ears.

Contrary to popular belief, moles do not eat tulip bulbs, or any other plant; they are carnivores/insectivores. In fact, their diet of grubs and underground insects, added to their habit of mixing the soil, is beneficial to plants.

Unfortunately, in digging out bugs, they can unintentionally damage the roots of your ornamentals. Plus, myriad other creatures -- including meadow voles and mice, who do indeed eat plants -- make free use of the moles' hard-wrought tunnels, and it often seems that the more expensive the plant, the tastier it is.

Nor are moles nocturnal; in fact, unlike most critters, they don't coordinate their daily rhythm with the sun's cycle at all. Instead, they tend to lie low when they sense movement nearby, and become active when everything is quiet. Around human habitations, it's quietest at night; thus, in the morning folk discover fresh tunnels and assume the culprit is nocturnal.

True mammals, female moles nurse their young, raising one litter of two to six pups per year. After about three months, the young moles disperse, making their own new tunnels.

They don't hibernate, nor can they store insects the way chipmunks do seeds, so they dig through your yard all winter, constantly looking for worms and insects. One five-ounce mole can eat up to fifty pounds of bugs a year.

Moles manage to avoid most of the predators that like to eat small mammals by remaining below ground. Hawks can't see them, and cats generally don't want to get their paws dirty by digging. Unfortunately, many dogs, like Arthur, can and will dig at the slightest provocation, without any apparent concern for personal cleanliness.

So "Drop it" is a handy command to have in your dog's vocabulary.

Trying to pry a toy from your dog's mouth with brute strength only demonstrates to both of you that he can defiantly hang onto something you want. Unless you have a Yorkie or some other tiny breed, Fido is more likely to win this battle of wills than you are -- and even if you do get the toy away from him, the dog probably had a great time fighting you for it.

Another variation on this frustrating theme is the dog who will chase a ball and bring it *almost* back, but won't give it to you. Again, playing "keep-away" is an exhilarating game, for the dog.

The trick is to make your dog want to give up the toy. How? Simple: offer something better.

First, you need a small amount of bacon or ham, cut into dime-sized pieces. Using your dog's favorite toy, play tuggie with him. Really get into it, laughing and pulling for a few minutes. Then suddenly let go. In a serious tone, use his name and tell him to "Drop it" (or whatever command you prefer) -- then show him the piece of bacon.

If he's a normal, healthy canine, he'll drop the toy in order to gulp the bacon. Praise him! Repeat this scene until he spits out the toy even before he sees the bacon. When he does, give him two or three pieces one right after another, heaping on the praise and petting. End the session with more play, and your dog will always love training time.

With just a few minutes of this a day, your dog will quickly learn to spit out whatever he's got in his mouth the instant you give the command, or even when you silently hold out your hand.

Nor must you always have a treat; random rewards can be more effective than giving him a goodie every time. If occasionally there is no treat, the dog might conclude that he didn't spit the toy out fast enough, and next time he'll try harder.

Eventually you won't need a treat at all -- and when he brings home a dead mole like Arthur did, he'll give it to you without hesitation. Try to pretent that you're pleased, instead of completely grossed out by the warm, wet corpse in your bare hand.

Arthur Sees a Painted Turtle at Dryden Lake

Saturday's crisp temperatures only served to energize my young Golden Retriever. He ran in circles for a bit after his morning ablutions, and then I decided it would be a great day to take him back to the trail by Dryden Lake.

Before leaving, I threw sticks for Arthur to take the edge off his over-abundant enthusiasm, in hopes that he would be able to walk at heel without too much nagging. The command starts out as, "Arthur, at heel," but after 56,712 repetitions, I've usually pared it down to a low, quiet, "at," and Arthur realigns himself at my side -- until the next distraction. They say goldfish have a three-second memory; sometimes Arthur isn't much better.

To be fair, I was distracted by our glorious surroundings, too: the slowly-thawing woods, the reappearing wildlife, the half-frozen lake. I tossed a small rock out to see how thick the ice on the lake was; the rock bounced once, then skittered for several yards, startling a small bird in the shore grasses. A little further on, a Great Blue Heron suddenly lifted from the weedy beach, flapping its great wings in a slow rhythm, reminding me of a pterodactl with its impressive size and majesty.

The ground was a bit muddy in places, and I tried to steer Arthur clear of the worst spots, wincing as he plopped his big paws smack into a puddle as if completely unaware when I missed one. Hopefully the mud would dry and fall off before we got back to the car.

But it was on the way back that we got the biggest surprise: a medium-sized Painted Turtle swimming slowly in a large shallow pool on the other side of the trail from the lake. His lazy dog-paddle lent the illusion that he was walking along the bottom. I guess I expected turtles to use a fast, symmetrical swimming stroke like frogs, but this little guy's unhurried left-right movement was deceptively effective. Even though we stood right there watching, several times we lost sight of him in the clear water.

The most common type of turtle in our state, the aptly-named Painted Turtle sports distinctive red and yellow markings on its dark-green head and neck, which we could see clearly when he came up to the surface and poked his face out to breathe, and perhaps look around. It certainly appeared that he was eyeing us with wary disapproval from the safety of his little lagoon.

In warmer weather, these turtles are often seen basking on logs and rocks near the shores of lakes and ponds. They eat algae, aquatic plants, earthworms, mosquito larvae, tadpoles and carrion, playing an important role in the ecosystem. (Personally, I applaud anyone who eats mosquitoes.)

Fascinating turtle facts: their gender is determined by the temperature of the nest after the eggs have been laid -- cooler incubation results in mostly males, warmer, mostly females. A group of turtles is called a "bale." Turtles live on every continent except Antarctica. The Musk turtle emits a foul odor when threatened. The first recognizable turtles existed 200 million years ago, and had teeth. An adult Speckled Padloper measures only four inches long, while the Leatherback sea turtle can grow up to ten feet. Turtles have keen eyesight and can see in full color. They have excellent hearing, and their shells have feeling. A turtle cannot stick his tongue out at you. Turtle shells are part of their skeleton, with the top shell made up of about 50 bones. Some females can produce viable eggs up to four years after mating. The red-footed tortoise native to South America can chirp and cluck like a chicken. On level ground, North America's smooth-shelled turtle can outrun a human.

Amazingly, although cold-blooded creatures, our Painted Turtles can survive months of winter temperatures by burying themselves in the mud at the bottom of the lake, the cold drastically reducing their need for oxygen. According to one study done in Michigan (the Painted Turtle is their state reptile), these humble turtles, the favorite of many a child (and adult!) may live up to sixty years.

I gave the turtle a nod of admiration, and finally we continued on our way, leaving it to its own agenda.

With a blend of relief, pride and triumph, I noted that Arthur's feet were almost completely clean as he jumped lightly into the back of the vehicle. It was only after I lifted him out when we got home, that he headed straight for the solitary two-foot by eight-inch mud puddle in the yard, and before I could call him back, he squelched right through with all four feet.

Arthur Almost Meets Some Canada Geese

This afternoon at Lucille's, over a hundred big Canada Geese settled in the cornfield across the street. These are the familiar harbingers of Fall when they fly south, and Spring when they return. So what were they doing here smack in the middle of the winter?

The originators of the goose-down coat, these birds also pack on a layer of insulating fat beneath that waterproof plumage, so it isn't the cold that drives them south; it's the scarcity of food and lack of open water. But not all Canada geese migrate.

These geese thrive and actually seem to prefer living in the suburbs, where only loose dogs pose any sort of threat, and all but the largest dogs would be unwise to annoy a flock of geese. Also, people feed them: either deliberately, as a hobby or form of entertainment (and the geese enjoy this as much or more than the humans), or accidentally, as when farmers harvest corn with machinery, which leaves a small percentage of crop in the field.

Canada geese are herbivores, eating grains, berries -- and grass. The close-cropped, tender lawns of suburbia, combined with ornamental and recreational ponds, have resulted in some geese choosing to remain all winter in parks, golf courses, and airports, where they can become a nuisance: a relatively small flock of just fifty geese will produce two and a half tons of guano a year. The same geese come back year after year; these are highly social birds, and if a family overwinters comfortably, the parents will return, along with last year's youngsters and occasionally unrelated flockmates as well.

Canada geese live and travel in family groups; watch carefully as a big flock comes in, and you can see how they break off into smaller groups as they land. The genders look alike (at least to us), but the male has a lower, slower call. During the nesting season, the male fiercely guards the nest even from other geese, while his mate does all the incubating. After the eggs hatch, however, the male relaxes towards his flockmates, and the chicks of several pairs sometimes gather together in a group called a creche, looked after by all the parents taking turns, rather like a gosling version of day care.

A wild Canada goose can live about twenty-four years. With a wingspan of up to six feet and a body weight anywhere from seven to twenty pounds, these beautiful birds are found, at some point during the year, in all the contiguous states of the US and every Canadian province.

Most of them do migrate, and they are masters of long-distance flight, covering up to fifteen hundred miles from one dawn to the next, following generations-old traditional routes and usually stopping in the same places to eat and sleep from one year to the next.

The largest subspecies, native to the midwest, is called the Giant Canada Goose. It, like the Ivory-Billed Woodpecker, was once considered extinct, a victim of overhunting and habitat destruction. Then, in the 1960's a few isolated family groups were discovered, and the population is now considered stable, thanks to reintroduction programs and better game laws.

Arthur and I approached the peacably grazing geese slowly -- him, with alert curiosity, and me with wary caution. Some years ago, Lucille's father, Ed, encouraged me to catch a half-grown gosling, a feat which proved absurdly easy. What I hadn't anticipated (but he did) was that Mama Goose would erupt in a shrieking fury of maternal protection, clubbing me painfully with her surprisingly solid wings (aren't they hollow bones?) while trying to rip my face off with her four-inch serrated beak.

Forgetting that I still clutched the chick, whose screams infuriated his mom, I stumbled blindly into the car and slammed the door barely in time to avoid the militant mother's lunge.

Ed just laughed, having encountered an irritated goose or two in his time. Always glad to entertain, I ended up opening the window just far enough to gently toss the fuzzy baby out into the care of his aggrieved parent. Almost instantly Mom reverted to her previous placid personality, but I wasn't fooled. After that I've always treated geese with the respect they deserve.

Now, walking carefully down the driveway, I kept my hand on Arthur's noble head, ostensibly to lend him some self-discipline, but really to reassure myself that I wasn't about to get us both attacked by an angry mob. These geese had no chicks to defend; surely they wouldn't attack me and my innocent, trusting dog. I hoped.

As we neared the road, three or four geese flew up, followed by about half the flock -- noisily honking their disapproval of the interruption, spiraling out and away across the field.

Arthur watched in rapt entrancement. He has been taught to retrieve small, frozen game birds, but never anything that moved. With the self-confidence of his flawless heritage, he showed only intelligent interest in every line of his classic body, blissfully unaware of what a Canada goose could do to a dog. Nor will he ever find out.

After unintentionally chasing off the geese that Lucille had enjoyed admiring (and I still feel bad about that), we went back in, where Arthur let Lucille salve his unsatisfied curiosity with biscuits and petting. In moments his disappointment was forgotten; as Lucille fed him and made much of him, Arthur squirmed on his back with pleasure, messing up the rug. Again.

Arthur Enjoys a Non-Traditional Thanksgiving Dinner

Thanksgiving morning, I let Arthur out, and stood on the front step to supervise. He knows better than to head down the quarter-mile driveway without me, and politely refrains from eating the cat's food or annoying her. No, the main reason I stand shivering in my pajamas on the porch is to make sure he doesn't forget to do what he went out to do.

This may sound ridiculous, but he knows he gets fed as soon as he comes back in, and like most dogs, he loves to eat.

While this arrangement does replace any inclination to wander with a preference to wait impatiently right by the door, it isn't at all unusual for me to have to remind him point-blank to *go pee,* and the cat -- like most cats -- has some psychological aberrations that can make Arthur's wait uncomfortable.

She likes to purr and rub against his front legs, then without provocation or warning, hiss and cuff his face. Poor Arthur just stands there, head held high out of her reach, too civilized to defend himself against a creature so much smaller than himself.

Janette is a tiny longhaired calico, yet one more in a long series of anonymous donations. Such drop-offs are common to anyone living in the country, but few of these furry friends find good homes. Nor are domestic cats suited for life in the wild, particularly in Central New York, where winter temperatures can drop past minus twenty, rabies is a constant threat, and coyotes are abroad and hungry.

The solution, of course, is for every pet owner to spay or neuter their cat (or dog.) Not only would this spare innumerable puppies and kittens a short, miserable life, but these procedures also actually prevent some forms of cancer and other health problems in your animal companion.

So there I was on Thanksgiving morning, making sure Arthur accomplished everything he had to do. Then I followed him back in, only to regret it moments later.

"Wooftracks!" I yelled, hopping on one foot, having stepped directly into a muddy puddle left by one of his big fuzzy feet. That command freezes Arthur where he is, to give me a chance to wipe his feet before he paw-prints the entire floor. This time I also reached for the scissors.

"Can't watch the Thanksgiving Day dog show with Dr. Seuss feet," I admonished, as I trimmed the fur on his toes, top and bottom. When Arthur was properly barbered and brushed, I got dressed and we went to Lucille's for dinner, and to see who would win this year's Best In Show trophy.

As always, we rooted for the Golden Retriever, although this year I have to say I've seen better-looking dogs here in Cortland than the one representing the breed on the televised program.

The other afternoon we met a beautiful Golden walking with his human across from the hospital, and Riley had a longer and richer-colored coat than the dog in the show, plus a sweet, friendly temperament to match.

Arthur was not the slightest bit interested in watching the dogs on the television, except to softly woof back when he heard barking.

My dear friend Lucille doesn't object to the fact that I've never quite outgrown the pleasure of sitting on the living room floor to eat and watch television. Arthur, of course, approves wholeheartedly of this deplorable habit, and when I set aside my plate, that's his cue to come drape himself over my legs, or pester Lucille for petting.

But until I'm done, he lays several feet away, avoiding even eye contact. It drives me nuts to have a dog lay there eyeing the fork while I eat, following it from plate to mouth, groaking and drooling hopefully.

"Go lay down," I'll tell him redundantly, and he gives a deep, resigned sigh and rolls onto one shoulder, facing away. He knows that when I say that phrase in that tone, it means no one is going to feed him, or even pay attention to him.

The hardest part to teaching this command is for everyone involved to follow through, every time. Say it once, like you mean it, and then everybody in the room must consistently ignore the dog. At first, don't ask him to wait more than thirty seconds or so, and when he does that successfully, gradually extend the time until he can leave you in peace for an entire meal.

This shouldn't be too difficult for your chum to learn, as it's instinctive for subordinate pack members to wait until the dominant individuals finish eating before they approach. Making your dog observe this form of respect is one more way of quietly reinforcing your role as the leader.

The ideal time to start this training is when you first get your dog, regardless of his age. It's always much easier to teach good habits than break bad ones, but it's never too late to tackle any problem, especially if your dog's behavior annoys you. Remember, he wants to please you.

After you leave the table, always make a point of releasing him with a specific word or phrase, and invite him over for praise and petting, and maybe a treat.

Arthur savored each tiny piece he was given of Lucille's scrumptious Thanksgiving pot roast. It takes a truly terrific friend to flout tradition and make my favorite meal instead of turkey on Thanksgiving.

Thanks, Lucille!

Even Arthur Considers Our Latest Snowfall a bit Much

This weekend the snow finally got too deep for my six-year-old Golden Retriever to enjoy running circles around the house. Oh, he'll gladly galumph out into the deepest drifts if I throw a frisbee (or a snowball, if I'm in the mood to flaunt my superior intellect by tricking a dog), but most of the yard is now higher than his shoulders, and he has to move in a series of ridiculous-looking hops, reminding me of little Pepper, a friend's dog weighing a tenth of Arthur's eighty pounds, who had to do jackrabbit jumps to get around in less than a foot of the white stuff.

That's not to say Arthur doesn't still enjoy going outside -- I not only clear the driveway, but also several paths, and Arthur pads up and down these tunnels, checking for signs of other critters, and leaving his own. Unfortunately, Arthur turns delirious with anticipation whenever I pull my boots on, and has to be told, "Nice!" each and every time I open the door, or he explodes out the door in a flurry of fur and snow in his haste to run and have fun, with a blithe disregard for the safety of his human companion.

Waiting to be allowed out is a pleasant courtesy -- and a simple command to train, because most household dogs already regard their owner as the beloved alpha of the family, and with zero training will automatically get out of your way if you walk toward them.

Taking advantage of this natural inclination, all you have to do is stand silently between the dog and the door for five to ten seconds, enough to establish that you occupy that space. Crowd toward him if need be, to make him give you elbow room, and the dog will likely respect you enough to remain in place even when you open the door, with no comment or command from you other than your confident presence. Eye contact is not necessary; act like you take for granted that your dog will not plow through you (as you have every right to expect), and generally they won't. If not, reinforce it by telling him to "Sit, stay" and wait until he does so.

Once you've established this few seconds to give your dog's rational mind a chance to regain control over brainless excitement, take your time stepping through the door yourself (or just move aside if you're in your pajamas and it's twelve degrees outside), then say calmly and firmly, "Nice." Remember that yelling will not calm your dog down; a quiet, assertive voice is far more effective. Chances are, those few moments of enforced stillness defused his firecracker compulsion, and he can now walk quietly out without knocking anyone over or bashing a dent in the screen door. (Don't ask.)

Coming back in, do the same thing. Consistency is key. Every time you open a door, make him acknowledge that you get to go through first, or that he needs your explicit permission to precede you. When I bring him back inside, we stay on the porch while I wipe Arthur off and clean his feet, so he doesn't leave a trail of melted snow puddles for me to step in unsuspecting.

Saturday I played with Arthur in the snow, trying to exhaust him enough that he'd be content to nap for the rest of the afternoon.

Yep, that worked about as well as you'd expect. As thrilled that I was joining him as if I hadn't risked hypothermia to play with him just twelve hours earlier, Arthur danced around, snatching mouthfuls of snow and sneezing, then running madly toward me like a locomotive, skidding to a stop at the very last second, getting snow in my boots.

When we were ready to go back in, Arthur was a mess from chasing snowballs in the deep drifts, shoving his blocky, bearlike head into the snow to snorfle for interesting scents, and making doggy snow angels, working the snow deep into his shaggy gold coat. I towelled him off, then worked on his feet, my fingers turning numb as I picked ice balls out from between his toes. Later, I'd have to trim his feet again.

In case you foolishly decide to attempt to exhaust your own dog into somnolence, remember that an exuberant retriever in the prime of life has way more stamina than a sleep-deprived 44-year-old woman. I was the one who ended up napping, while Arthur padded around, cheerfully pestering the cat.

Arthur Enjoys the Benefits of Cold Winter Weather

The overnight change from mild October temperatures to weather more appropriate for mid-January turned my yard from a morass of mud to pristine snow and ice. While I hate the cold, I'm also relieved, because a golden retriever can carry an unbelievable amount of mud in that fuzzy coat, and my poor chum has never quite made the connection that when he's clean, he gets to go all sorts of fun places with me, like the bank and the feed store (well, *he* thinks they're fun); dirty, he remains exiled outside in the Jeep.

One of Arthur's most cherished activities is breakfast at Lucille's, where he delights in lavish affection and buttered toast crusts. However, he can't come in if he's liberally covered in mud. Trouble is, after being cooped up in the house all night, Arthur needs to expend some energy. For him, this means high-speed laps around the yard, with an occasional exuberant roll. The recent freeze provided us a handy solution to the mud problem, but now there's snow, which accumulates in his coat and then leaves puddles of ice water on the floor inside as it melts from his fur. While we do have our own towel in Lucille's garage, still, it's easier if he just stays clean and dry in the first place, and he gets more time to bask in her attention if we don't have to waste ten minutes cleaning up out on the steps.

So the other day I was glad to see the snow, even though I could also see my breath in the air. Standing in the first rays of sunrise, I considered Arthur for a moment, as he dashed madly back and forth through the snow. I still had to feed the birds, and reluctantly cut his fun short and sent him back to the house while I did so. It wasn't that I didn't want him with me; it's just that he would acquire another pound or so of snow in his coat in the five minutes it would take me to dump some sunflower seeds in the feeder.

"Arthur, go home," I told him, as I took down the suet cage and opened a fresh brick of suet.

Delighted at this opportunity to do something for me, Arthur turned and immediately galumphed across the front yard to go sit on the porch in front of the door, his thick tail sweeping the wooden planks.

This command, while vaguely reminiscent of Timmy and Lassie, is much more than a convenient way to keep Arthur clean. No matter where we are in the surrounding countryside, I can send him home and know he will go straight there, and wait patiently for me to return and praise him. Nobody does reliability like a golden who knows he'll be praised.

Teaching this command depends on being predictable. Every time I headed for the house, I told Arthur to "go home," and eventually he began to race me there when I said it. The instant his feet hit the porch, I yelled, "EXCELLENT!" then told him to sit and stay, and made him wait for me.

When he got good at this, I began to take my time, until now, instead of rebuking him for getting snow all over his coat, I can tell him to go home, and he does. (My roofless stoop does not, however, keep him dry when it's raining.)

It's much more productive to give your pup a command to prevent an annoying behavior, rather than simply telling him you're annoyed. A command immediately alters the offending behavior, and you get to praise him instead of getting mad. Because even I sometimes get mad at Arthur. Ninety-nine percent of the time he's so well-behaved, that when he slips up and acts like a normal dog that one percent, it always takes me by surprise.

Scolding merely informs your dog that you're angry; it doesn't give him any clue how to modify his behavior to make peace. When, for instance, Arthur goes into lunatic mode while being petted, I don't tell him he's bad. I just make him sit-stay, or better yet, stand-stay, because he's not deliberately disobeying; he just gets too excited.

The B-word I reserve for serious offenses. where Arthur knowingly chooses to flout the rules in favor of immediate personal gratification -- like that time he ate curly fries out of the takeout bag when I left him alone in the Jeep with it. He didn't touch them while I pumped gas, but then I disappeared into the building to pay. When I came back out, there he was with the cardboard box wedged on his snout, as he struggled to reach the last few fries at the bottom. (And yes, I cheerfully ate the few that I managed to save.)

Whenever your canine companion misbehaves, you are always at least partially to blame. In this case, I had been eating fries as I drove, and feeding Arthur pieces. Nor am I even sure he grasped that what he did was wrong, since laughing while reprimanding him kind of spoiled the effect. Next time I'll leave the the takeout bag on the hood while I'm gone.

Arthur and the Holidays

From a Golden Retriever's point of view, the holidays really aren't as much fun as we seem to think they are. There are visitors Arthur is forbidden to pester for attention, new items around the house that he mustn't pick up and carry around, and scrumptious foods he can smell but isn't allowed to eat. So far he's managed to get through the excitement of Halloween and Thanksgiving with his "Good Puppy" status intact; now he just has Christmas and New Year's to go.

(A note here on the variability of dog years. Every well-behaved canine, regardless of age, is a "Good Puppy." Anytime they're bad, even if they're only a couple months old, they're a "Bad Dog." This helps make approval and disapproval sound distinctly different to your chum.)

In addition to the many disappointments your dog is bound to experience, the holidays can be downright dangerous. Most decorations are not meant to be eaten or chewed. Make sure nothing you put within reach can harm your furry family member -- and this long list includes poisons like chocolate, decorations and ornaments that can be broken or swallowed, plus other dangers like hot stoves and fireplaces, and open doors.

Be careful of visitors coming in and going out; if they're not used to a dog in the house, they might not remember they have to be careful to keep Fido in. During this season of travel, there tends to be more traffic on even the most rural roads, and drivers might not be paying as much attention as they normally would. Some dogs wander off and in all the hubbub, nobody notices they're gone until they're lost, and some pets never find their way back home.

Sometimes visitors bring dogs of their own. I've never felt it necessary for pets to socialize. Unless they know each other and get along, it's best for everyone to separate them. Introducing two strange dogs on the home turf of one during a time of food smells, general confusion and human distraction is just asking for trouble. I can't help but remember poor little Max, a tiny black poodle that Arthur's 80-pound uncle accidentally stepped on when Max dived under Hobby to try to grab a toy. Max suffered a dislocated shoulder and elbow, and spent weeks in a body wrap.

And then there are children. Never, never leave a child with a pet unsupervised. Even the sweetest, most trustworthy dog can be clumsy, or get excited. One Golden Retriever tragically killed a young girl by playing tuggie with her scarf. On the other hand, children are not always as gentle as they should be with animals, and nobody wants to spend Christmas at the vet's office, including the vet.

But the holidays aren't all gloom and doom for our canine chums, either. When I brush him and dress him up in some silly outfit, Arthur revels in the extra attention. Get some high-quality dog biscuits, so he doesn't feel quite so deprived. Sure, he can smell roast beef and gravy, and the biscuit tastes like, well, dog food, but Arthur sure doesn't hesitate to gulp it down.

I like getting the small size biscuits, and then break them in half. Despite Arthur's ability to derive square roots, he doesn't seem to have a good grasp of geometry. He inhales most treats whole, so he really only knows that he got a snack. I even have my doubts he knows with any degree of certainty *what* he just ate, especially if I make him do a trick first and get him all wacky with praise. (Back before the manufacturer began making heartworm pills taste good, that's how I tricked Hobby into taking them.)

And above all, during the holidays is when most people take time off work to spend with family at home, and more than food or toys or anything else in this world, your dog just wants to be with you.

Arthur and I wish everyone, furry and non-furry alike, a happy and safe holiday season!

Arthur Helps Identify Hyperactive
Red Squirrel Tracks

One great thing about snow (besides hiding roadside litter and the neighbor's yard junk) is wildlife tracks. Last Saturday, Arthur and I went out into the woods to see who had been doing what.

As usual, the big, fuzzy retriever danced in circles around me, delighted we were going on a romp together. Normally I'm enchanted by his joyous affection, but now he was obliterating a line of tiny handprints stitched delicately across the surface of the snow.

"Arthur, get away!" I told him.

It's hard to dampen a golden's gladness. Ever obedient, but with good mood intact, Arthur ranged a few yards out from me, stopping every few feet to thrust his face into the snow, snorting and sneezing, while I followed the tracks and tried to identify the woodland denizen by the signs they left. A two-foot-wide pile of pinecone pieces at the base of a big white pine told me that I have at least one resident red squirrel -- no big surprise, as I see them fighting on and around the feeder every day.

Red squirrels are the hyperactive, feisty version of their larger, gray cousins. Also called chickarees, these rodents are diurnal: awake and active during the day. One of their staple foods is pine cones, which they like to take to a favorite eating spot, such as a tree branch or stump with a good view, and systematically strip the scales from the shaft to get at the nutritious seeds, leaving a signature midden heap of discards below.

Red squirrels also cut conifer branches a few inches from the ends to get at the tender buds, leaving tell-tale nip twigs on the ground, and of course they cheerfully take full advantage of a birdfeeder, often holding it against all comers. Only the arrival of someone larger or more aggressive, such as a hairy woodpecker or a group of bluejays, will send them skittering high into the bare branches above, with an angry retort and lashing tail -- but not for long.

Chickarees are one of the few squirrels who make tunnels beneath the snow, usually two to four inches wide. However, they can and will squeeze through a hole just an inch and a half in diameter, especially if it's warmer on the other side. These canny little critters have adapted so well to human development that they may even come right inside your house and make free with your cupboards.

When my nose was finally cold enough to freeze inside with every inhale, I called Arthur off whatever he was tracking, and we went back inside to thaw out. I toed off my boots as Arthur padded across the kitchen and flopped on the floor, tired and satisfied. An exhausted retriever is a happy retriever, and Arthur was ecstatic.

An ice ball crunched beneath my unsuspecting sock-clad foot. Arthur had smuggled in four fully-furred paws' worth of snow, and in my toasty-warm cabin, it was turning into invisible ice water mines. Well, whose fault was that?

Getting the scissors from the drawer, I sat down beside my somnolent dog and clipped the fur on his feet, not just between his pads, but the tops too, giving him a natty show-dog look. Toenails were next; then, because the floor was already a mess of dog hair, bits of nail, and snow melt, I decided it was a good time to trim the inside of his ears as well.

All dogs benefit from regular home ear care in addition to the thorough cleaning they get at their yearly visit to the vet. Dogs with floppy ears or long hair are especially appreciative of this important bit of grooming.

Left untouched, the wax and fur can build up into an infection inside the ear canal, which is painful and smelly, and can cause permanent hearing damage.

There are roughly eight million different products on the market for cleaning your dog's ears. I use a simple solution recommended by the vet: equal parts water and vinegar. I apply a little of this to a soft paper towel wrapped over my finger and carefully wipe the wax out of his ears. I use a paper towel rather than a cotton swab because it gives me better control when I can feel what I'm doing. A small flashlight helps, too.

Slow and gentle are the key. If it's done right, most dogs don't mind having their ears cleaned, and many, like Arthur, genuinely enjoy ear scrubbles. He leeeeeans into me and moans softly. I kid you not.

After sweeping up the kitchen, I sat on the floor and hauled Arthur's big blocky head and lion's-mane shoulders onto my lap for smooches, smiling as his fuzzy tail thumped the floor in a drowsy rhythm which slowed and then stopped as he gradually fell asleep. Quietly I slid his head back onto the floor without waking him, and stood, glancing out the window at the birds.

The feeders were empty; only the suet remained, and the smaller birds flitted about, hungry but wary of the big woodpecker who had laid claim to the suet.

With a chuckle, I pulled on my boots to go put more sunflower seed out for the chickadees and chickarees.

Why Arthur Avoids Porcupines

Mornings aren't as much fun when they start while it's still dark. Before I can let Arthur outside, I have to peer into the pitch-black front yard to make sure I'm not letting him gallop into a confrontation with any sort of wildlife.

Arthur isn't prone to chasing any of our timid furry woodland neighbors; it's the ones who aren't scared of him that he needs to avoid startling: skunk, for instance, or porcupines.

On the wall at the vet's, I recently spotted a photo of a dog who had the misfortune to encounter a porcupine. The poor little pup was a mess.

Sometimes it seems that if a dog annoys a porcupine and gets smacked with a few quills, the pain escalates the dog's aggression, spurring her into a serious attack. It then requires a veterinarian to anesthetize the dog to remove hundreds of quills, even from inside her mouth, because the barbs on each quill pull it deeper into the dog until it comes out the other side -- assuming it doesn't kill the dog on the way through.

The dog in the photo was lucky; her owner took her to the vet right away, so she didn't suffer any lasting damage, or spend any longer than necessary enduring the agony of those quills. But it got my attention, because I didn't think porcupines were particularly plentiful in Central New York. As it turns out, porcupines can be found throughout the New England states, New York, and most of Pennsylvania, plus a large section of the western United States, Alaska, and parts of Canada.

These slow-moving rodents spend a good deal of their time in trees. In the winter, they den up, subsisting mostly on nuts and the bark of conifers and hardwoods. Come spring, the sweet buds of maples and other trees are a favorite. In summer they add various field greens and flowers to their vegetarian menu.

Averaging between seven and fifteen pounds (although extremely large individuals might weigh as much as forty pounds!), a porcupine sports around thirty thousand quills. Despite this impressive armament, porcupines are generally pacifistic, although there are cases where they initiated hostilities by slapping an over-curious dog in the face with their tail. They are fearless for a very good reason, and you don't want your dog to meddle with one.

Every morning as soon as Arthur comes back in, he heads straight for his crate. It never hurts to have your dog comfortable being in a crate and happy to dive in on command. Locking him in his crate to eat makes teaching this a pleasant task, and also helps keep other household pets from taking over his food. If I feed Arthur in the middle of the kitchen floor and one of my other animals approaches, Arthur will immediately back away from his own half-eaten meal -- not because he fears the other critter, but because I have taught him that if he goes into his crate and lets the other pet have his dry food, I will not only feed him special goodies in his crate, I'll also replace the kibble when the other pet is done.

This is how I maintain peace in my home.

One big drawback to feeding him inside his crate was that I have to crawl almost completely inside the crate myself in order to put the bowl in and get it back, twice a day, every day. (Left in the front of the crate, Arthur dumps it trying to get inside. He's beautiful, not graceful.) Finally in a flash of inspiration I said to myself, "Wait a minute. He's a retriever, let him retrieve it."

Getting your dog to carry his dish requires first and foremost an unbreakable dish, preferably one with something a dog can easily get a grip on, like a lip around the top rim. Most dogs will readily pick up plastic, and plastic bowls are pretty sturdy. Arthur's happens to be stainless steel, but I had already accustomed him to the feel of metal in his mouth by feeding him off the tableware (I kid you not; this is a professional training trick.)

Choosing a good dish is the toughest part; after that, it's mostly merely a matter of letting your dog sniff a piece of roast beef, pointing to his bowl, then saying his name and "bring me your bowl" or whatever phrase you use for the command to retrieve. I say "bring" instead of "fetch" because I prefer speaking to Arthur in conversational tones, such as quietly saying, "Arthur, bring me my keys from the counter," instead of bellowing, "Fetch! Keys! Counter!" It just sounds nicer. Besides, dogs possess excellent hearing; if you need to yell to get your dog's attention, you might want to reevaluate your training methods.

The more terms your dog knows, the easier it is for him to learn new ones.

In a matter of minutes, Arthur mentally attached the word "bowl" to the desired object, and added it to his ever-growing vocabulary. Now he'll search for his bowl whenever I ask, which comes in handy before mealtime, too: I simply stand next to the box where I keep his food and ask him to bring his bowl, and he delivers it with a resounding clang (unlike frisbees or plush toys, he can't seem to hang onto his bowl until I take it, and kind of throws it at me instead.)

The only problem with this new method is that when he can't find his food bowl right away, he's so eager to produce it that he sometimes grabs his matching water dish instead.

Mornings are especially not fun when you start them off by mopping up half a gallon of water, but on the up side, my kitchen floor is spotless.

Arthur Encounters a Killdeer

This is the time of year when farmers work long and hard to plow and plant their yearly crops, leaving flat fields of fresh earth -- and muddy detritus on the roads. Unfortunately for people who walk on the side of these roads (especially those of us with big furry dogs) some of it isn't mud at all, but locally-produced organic fertilizer, fresh from the barn floor. Lots of it. Great.

The dirt road I take Arthur up is normally dotted with mud puddles here and there, but on Sunday it was a veritable mine field of stuff I would've preferred to avoid entirely, and which my Golden Retriever found irresistibly fascinating. Having long since resigned myself to hosing his feet and belly off in the yard when we got home, I mentally added soap to this future project, and let him investigate, although I drew the line at allowing him the pleasure of doing a doggy "stop, drop and roll" as he clearly yearned to do.

Suddenly, from one of the freshly-seeded fields beside us, a small, highly excited, pointy-tailed, brown-and-white bird came shrieking and fluttering out to flop around in front of us as we walked, to all appearances hopelessly injured and unable to fly, yet somehow always managing to stay safely beyond the reach of the leashed dog. Arthur was instantly riveted, focusing intently on this Academy Award-worthy performance, oblivious (as the bird intended) of the small, shallow depression in a tiny, untilled patch of the field, in which lay hidden her four speckled eggs.

The killdeer is a member of the plover family of long-legged wading birds, named for the distinctive two-note call that apparently sounded like someone saying "kill-deer" to the rather imaginative naturalists of the eighteenth century. Killdeer are slender birds, tawny on top with a white belly, that are only in our area for the summer breeding season, spending their winters as far south as Central America. Adult males and females look similar, with two black bands at their neck, and a pale "eyebrow" patch. (Juveniles have only one black throat band.) When looking for food, they typically run a few feet, then stop and check for any insects they've scared up.

Technically classified as a shorebird, killdeer are equally comfortable on beaches, airports, fields, and golf courses, where they forage the short-mown vegetation for worms and insects. Well-known for the "broken-wing" display they use to lure predators away from their eggs; but when their nest is imperiled by a clumsy cow's hooves, they stand their ground and fluff themselves up, screaming that piercing cry, and even running toward the unwitting offender to make it change direction.

Many farmers notice killdeer nests, and mark them with a flag like the one we saw, so they can avoid plowing them under. I smiled at this particular unknown individual, who was either simply very kind, or perhaps understood the balance of Nature well enough to know that the killdeers' voracious appetite for insects probably saves more corn or hay than what he might have gotten from the six square feet of land he sacrificed in order for these beneficial little birds to hatch and raise their young undisturbed.

Just as suddenly as it had appeared, the killdeer made a miraculous recovery about fifty yards from her nest, and flew up and away, completely baffling my poor dog. Arthur, his brain flooded with generations of instinct handed down from his hunting and retrieving ancestors, just couldn't believe it. That bird had been practically his! He snuffled at the hard-packed earth where she had taken flight, then looked up at me, his tail waving uncertainly at half-mast, asking with his soulful brown eyes what he'd done wrong.

"You're a good puppy," I reassured him, petting his silky golden head, and his metronome tail resumed its normal happy wag, the missed prey forgotten as he basked in my approval. It's easy to make a dog happy. We turned and headed home.

The weather had threatened rain all day, but we only got a hot, muggy wind. The mud (and other stuff) on him conveniently dried and fell off long before we got home, with no effort on my part. He took a long drink from the water bowl, then flopped over on his side on the cool kitchen floor and slept, doubtless dreaming of catching shorebirds.

Arthur Enjoys a Visit from a Neighbor

After one of the recent rains, the grass was wet with mud beneath, so I kept an eagle eye on my Golden retriever as we went out to get a book from the car. He would need his feet wiped before we went back inside, but that was what the old towel in the breezeway was for, and it was a small price to pay for the joy it gave him to tag along. Even a two-minute walk outside with their human is an exciting jaunt to a dog.

He stood panting, gazing wistfully at the lawn. He wanted to roll, I could see it in his eyes, but I knew he wouldn't. I got the novel from the passenger seat, just as Arthur gave a deep woof.

"Arthur, stay," I told him. It was one of our neighbors, an elegant older woman who had an old chocolate Lab that we saw only infrequently. She stopped, and we chatted a bit.

Throughout our conversation, Arthur remained in sit-stay, although trembling all over in his excitement. Then our neighbor said, quietly and sorrowfully, that she had to have her dog put to sleep a week ago. She was looking at Arthur, not me, and I knew from personal experience that a canine hug would be more consoling than anything I could offer by way of sympathy.

She took a few steps toward Arthur, and I softly said, "Okay."

Before I could guess his intentions, Arthur hurled his eighty-pound self at the woman, planting his muddy feet on her exquisite red coat. I cringed. "Arthur!"

Fortunately, our graceful neighbor is made of surprisingly sturdy stuff. Unperturbed at this sudden assault, she petted him and murmured to him, then calmly took a step back and he dropped to all fours.

In an effort to convince her that Arthur isn't as demented as he appeared, I told her that he can open the car door. This is a fairly easy thing to teach a dog, but marvellously dramatic. I unlocked the car, and Arthur dashed over, yanked the handle up with his teeth, then butted his head into the opening and leaped in, golden fur flashing in the sun.

"EXCELLENT!" I laughed, as he leaped out of the car for petting. I was so pleased and proud that I didn't even stop him when he happily dropped and rolled, digging the mud deep into his thick coat. When he finally stood up to shake, even the top of his head was brown.

But it was worth it. Our elegant neighbor was impressed with how smart he was, despite the muddy paw prints on her coat.

Arthur Enjoys Some Unintentional Training

Generally when we train dogs we deliberately modify their behavior, but sometimes it's entirely unintentional. Obvious rewards include things like a snack, a word of praise, or petting -- but something as subtle as remaining outside could also motivate your pup.

The difficulty in un-training a bad habit is that you can't just yell "No!" This tells the dog you're unhappy with him, but leaves him unable to guess how to please you. You have to provide an alternative acceptable behavior in place of the unwanted one.

If you walk your dog in the morning before going to work, from his point of view, it seems that as soon as he does his business, he's taken back inside and left alone all day. So while you're impatiently waiting, he's putting it off as long as he can. One way to break this habit is to praise him as soon as he goes, and maybe play with him for a few minutes afterwards. If you're in a hurry, even two or three frisbee throws will do. The important part is to make him happy immediately after he does something you want him to do.

Another time many people inadvertently encourage a vice is dinnertime. The first thing to teach any dog is that all food is yours. You might give him a bowl of kibble, but if you decide you want it back, he should let you have it without protest. Arthur takes this politeness one step further: he won't approach his own bowl until invited to do so.

Unfortunately, some folks feel they shouldn't interrupt a dog while he's eating, which unintentionally teaches the dog that humans will stand back until he's done. This is how lesser members of the pack would defer to the pack leader, and you do not want your dog to start thinking he is the pack leader.

If you have a puppy, the solution is simple: just pick his bowl up several times while he's eating, praise him and maybe put a treat on top of the food, like a small piece of ham, then give it back. Older dogs might be more of a challenge. Try not putting his bowl of food on the floor at all. Take it to another room and sit in a chair with it, with him on the floor. Handfeed him his dinner, piece by piece, and play with him afterwards. This leaves him with nothing to defend, and the act of eating from your hand makes him realize you are the provider.

Another variation on bad manners at dinnertime is begging. I've actually witnessed two dogs that barked incessantly at the dinner table, and to get them to be quiet for a few moments, their owners actually fed them people food off their own plates. To my dismay, one of these people feeds Arthur from her plate, when he crowds up against her while she's eating! To Arthur's credit, he seems instinctively aware that he should not try this at home.

Instead of rewarding bad behavior, try not giving your dog anything at all while you are eating, not even his own kibble. As I've said, the pack leaders eat first, unannoyed by the rest of the pack, who wait patiently and respectfully. You are the pack leader; step into this role with confidence. If your dog parks himself right next to you and stares at your fork while you're eating, tell him to go lay down. If necessary, take him to another room and put him in down-stay. Eventually he will learn that he's not getting anything until after you're done.

After the humans have finished and gotten up from the table, then give Fido his dog food, maybe with a teaspoon of gravy on top. (Dogs have a terrific sense of smell; a tiny amount of gravy is all that's needed, and too much isn't good for him.) Once the routine is established, dinnertime will be pleasant and peaceful, and you won't have that puddle of dog drool next to your chair.

By far the most important thing you can teach your dog is to come on command, instantly and reliably. One mistake that's easy to make is using your dog's name when you yell at him. That just makes him associate his name with being punished. Always, *always*, make coming to your hand a happy thing. Use a different version of his name when you're mad at him (much like your mother used your full name when you were in trouble as a kid) or something else entirely. When Arthur misbehaves (and he occasionally does) his name is Bad Dog.

But please, unless you can trust him one hundred percent to come when you call no matter whatever else might be going on, get a long leash and keep him safe. Those few moments of freedom aren't worth his life.

Arthur Walks Around Dryden Lake

Up until a few weeks ago, it had been over twenty years since I sat on a bicycle, but when I found myself in possession of an old one, I gamely hopped astride, hoping fervently that the adage about never forgetting how to ride a bike was true.

My faith in my abilities was such that I made my first foray across the nice soft lawn. To my pleased surprise, I managed to stay upright, and went more or less where I wanted to, but the finer points of coordination eluded me. Maybe it was the uneven turf, or maybe it was the crazy eighty-pound dog that apparently thought the bike was some exotic new dog toy I was throwing awkwardly for him.

I hadn't thought to tell my Golden Retriever to stay where he lay in the shade of the the big pine, because up until the moment I stepped onto the pedals, he had been flat on his side, to all appearances unconscious, possibly comatose. Turns out he's more aware of his surroundings than I gave him credit for.

Fortunately for me, I managed to convince him to just trot alongside without trying to help as I made my wobbly way across the yard. To him, I probably seemed to be having trouble holding onto the handlebars, and the whole thing would've looked like it was perilously close to getting away from me.

"Heel" is a wonderful command. If you only teach your dog one thing, this is the one to choose. In addition to combining *sit, stay* and *come* all rolled into one, it keeps your dog by your side as you walk or jog, or in this case, bicycle. Arthur's uncle Hobbes even understood how to pace at my horse's side when I went riding.

But could Arthur maintain such perfect heel position that I could take him with me biking on the quiet, unpaved trail around Dryden Lake, on a leash? What's the worst that could happen, he might tug at the wrong moment and send me and the bike to the ground? With no pavement and no cars to worry about, I decided the minimal danger to me was well worth the fun Arthur would have.

Off we went early the next morning, me packing two bottles of water for a two-mile leisurely ride, most of it for Arthur. In a helmet, jeans and long sleeves, I felt prepared for a spill or two. I called Arthur to heel and he obediently aligned himself with my left leg, even though I could tell he wanted to sniff around.

My comfortable biking speed was slow enough that one jogger actually passed us with a wave. We halted periodically in patches of shade, ostensibly for Arthur, but I sure didn't mind getting off the bike and catching my breath while I slowly poured water out of a bottle for Arthur. He's the only creature I know who can slurp while grinning.

Many dogs, like Arthur, can drink from a dribbling bottle, but unless you know for sure that your dog is good at this, bring along a dish as well as plenty of water. (If space is an issue, there are nifty collapsible bowls that fit nicely into a backpack.) Letting your chum drink from streams and lakes can be risky, because water with public access might contain broken glass and fishhooks, and may not be safe to drink.

On several of our rest stops, we spied the shiny shells of turtles dozing blissfully in the sun near the shore alongside the path, sometimes three and four to a log. Out further in the lake, huge carp swam in playful circles, occasionally surfacing and dancing on the water in a splashy display for a mate. We heard bullfrogs, and glimpsed an enormous silhouette flapping ponderously overhead, its long trailing legs identifying it as a heron.

I was very proud of my beautiful pup (yes, at seven years old, Arthur is still a puppy to me). He behaved like a perfect gentleman each time we encountered other people and dogs, and only twice did he come close to toppling me over. Once a tuft of grass distracted him momentarily, and on a bike, even at three miles per hour, having your handlebars yanked suddenly to the left on a rocky trail poses a serious challenge. I called him to heel with enough desperation that Arthur instantly trotted up alongside and I managed to correct my course before diving into the lake. I wasn't fooled by the sun; that water would've been chilly.

The second time I'll take the blame for. Although we stopped frequently, I never thought to give Arthur permission to go pee, and when he couldn't hold it anymore, he suddenly stopped and watered some wayside weeds. It's good to know the brakes work just fine on that old bike.

When we got home, I collapsed into a chair. Arthur had a big drink, then came over for yet more praise and petting (and to wipe his slobbery mouth on my jeans), then flopped down on the kitchen floor, content.

Arthur Looks for Lucille's Glove

It's been months since I last challenged my Golden Retriever with tracking, long enough that I had begun deliberately procrastinating out of fear he might have gotten rusty and end his lifetime 100% success rate at finding people and things. But finally I decided it was time to try him again, so I gave him the easiest test I could think of to re-introduce him to tracking and finding: I took him to my friend Lucille's.

Lucille's husband Larry keeps their several acres neatly mowed, making it an ideal dog-training course. I asked Lucille to choose a small, portable object that could get wet (although the weather was dry, Arthur's mouth is not.) She picked a purple glove, then we trooped outside.

I stood with Arthur in front of their garage so he couldn't see Lucille as she set off at her typical brisk pace, wandering around the backyard a bit before dropping the glove behind an evergreen and returning by a different path. Lucille has helped out with Arthur's training many times, and knows the drill.

Arthur, too, knows and quickly recognized the significance of sitting in the driveway with me while Lucille walked away on her own. His light panting deepened. He began to tremble with excitement, his thick furry ears propped up as high as they could go on his wide skull, and his golden brush swept the pavement clear of dead leaves with a *shush-shush-shush* sound.

When Lucille rejoined us, Arthur was holding himself in place, as taut as a violin string. Stiffly he managed to walk at heel until I pointed to the place where Lucille had started and said, "Arthur, find it."

I needn't have worried about his abilities fading with disuse. Off he took like a shot, snuffling around more or less where Lucille had just walked, until he pounced on the glove and then came straight for us, the thunder of his feet on the turf sounding more like a runaway horse than an eighty-pound dog.

The successful completion of his task, plus praise and petting way out of proportion for such a simple accomplishment, turned Arthur into an ecstatic idiot. He jumped and whirled, barely missing Lucille and me with his big muddy paws, until finally he calmed enough to release the purple glove into my hand, wadded-up and slime-soggy, but intact.

Emboldened by his casual display of a talent I can't comprehend, I got one of his toys out of my car, and made him sit-stay with Lucille in front of the garage while I hid it out back. Then we all went inside to watch a movie, letting the trail cool off for a couple of hours.

Just before we left, I pointed to where I'd begun my trip to hide the toy. As before, Arthur took off at an enthusiastic run, nose to ground, recreating my route (although I suspect his detour into the garden was purely for his own enjoyment) until he found the stuffed toy and brought it to me. His record remains perfect!

A warning to pet owners about pets and people food: on Thanksgiving, don't let Rover's soulful gaze of adoration play Jedi mind tricks on you, making you hand over slabs of roast turkey without thinking. He's not really in the final stages of death by starvation; that's an Academy Award-worthy performance he hones to perfection while you're not home (explaining those doggy nose prints in the mirror on the closet door.)

At best, you'll regret this "kindness" when your fuzzy chum sleeps near you later. As his gastrointestinal system struggles to deal with unaccustomed quantities of rich fare, the resulting effluvium (a euphemism for "horrifically stinky gas") will wake you, and possibly drive you retching from your own bedroom. The dog himself will cast a withering glance of surprise and accusation in your direction, and slink out of the room ahead of you.

At worst, suddenly giving Fido large amounts of fatty scraps (we all sneak little pieces to them now and then) could send his pancreas into overproduction and make it start digesting itself, an intensely painful condition. One of the first signs of pancreatitis is loss of appetite, so if your pup seems uncomfortable and refuses food when you know he isn't full, don't tempt him with further goodies. Call your veterinarian immediately! Some pets don't survive.

Of course, it's easier on you, your dog, and the vet if you don't overfeed your pet on people food. Trouble is, it can be terribly hard to resist. The best answer I've come up with is to keep a small dish of Arthur's normal dry dog food on the counter while I'm cooking, and periodically toss him a piece so he feels included in the festivities. It's sort of sneaky (smells like turkey, tastes like kibble) but he's never turned it down.

Arthur Tries Out an Electric Toothbrush

With all the recent rain, my Golden Retriever's luxurious coat, worthy of any show ring when dry and brushed and fluffy, isn't nearly as attractive sodden wet and decorated with grass clippings and mud from rolling around on the freshly-mowed lawn.

Nor did I want all of that in the house. Arthur stood patiently, front feet on the doorstep, soggy tail waving gently, as I lifted and dried off each foot one by one with the disreputable dog-towel, then briskly rubbed the towel back and forth down his sides from his head to his hips, and finished up with what he considered a belly-rub.

His tail wagged harder as I hung up the wet and heavy towel. Well, hopefully it would dry off before we needed it again in the morning. Stepping past him to open the door, I went in, then invited him in with a gesture. Happily he padded inside and went to look for a stuffed toy to carry around.

Drying off a wet dog will get you and at least one towel wet, although wetting down a dry dog doesn't get anything dry. I sat and pulled off my wet sweatshirt, only to discover that the t-shirt beneath was damp, too. Well, there's no law against taking a hot shower and pulling on self-indulgent flannel pajamas at 7:30 PM.

Half an hour later I was warm and dry again. I went over to the container of dog food, and Arthur politely laid down with his nose four feet from his food bowl. He watched, trembling in place as I dumped the scoop of kibble into the metal bowl, then he looked at me imploringly, his tail sweeping a fast arc on the floor. Fixing dinner for a dog is a real ego boost, even for the culinarily challenged.

When I said, "Okay," he leaped up and lunged for the food, gulping it down as if someone else might eat it if he didn't. Even though I choose high-quality dog food claiming it's "made with quality ingredients," I have no desire to sample it, and tell him so on a regular basis. But he never believes me.

After dinner, I curled up in my chair with a good book, not paying particular attention to Arthur until he wandered over to the water bowl and schlurped up a gallon or so, then turned his head and drooled at least half of that on the floor. Good thing I towelled him off to keep the floors dry.

Arthur ambled over to me and without warning, laid his big bearlike head down in my lap. I suspect he does this deliberately to dry off his mouth. My erstwhile cozy jammies soaked through in seconds, as Arthur looked up at me with his big soulful brown eyes, his whole back end wagging with the anticipation of being petted. When it comes to attention, Arthur is insatiable.

(Perhaps this is my fault; when I was a kid, we had a pet poodle who would only tolerate a certain amount of petting before stalking away -- and I wished, with all the fervor of childhood, for a dog who wanted to be petted more than I wanted to pet him. Too late I heard of the axiom, "Be careful what you wish for, you may get it.")

"Arthur, you're a good puppy, and I love you, but ..." I began. He lifted his head and looked at me hopefully, panting in anticipation of something fun. Arthur is a chronic optimist.

"But you have terrible breath!" I finished, standing. "Time to brush your teeth again." Arthur trotted alongside me as I went to get his nifty new toothbrush, a whimsical purchase after my dentist informed me that electric toothbrushes are much better at removing plaque, and I tried one. I saw no reason Arthur couldn't benefit from technology just as I did, and had no doubt that he would fully cooperate if I bribed him with playtime afterwards.

The first time I introduced him to this noisy, vibrating thing in his mouth, I expected to encounter some resistance on his part, but the reality was an utter anticlimax. He merely twitched his head a little to the side when I turned the brush on between his teeth and lips, then he held still as usual, no big deal. He trusts me so completely it's humbling.

The electric toothbrush does do a noticeably better job, allowing me to slack off and only brush his teeth two or three times a week to prevent that distinctive "doggy breath" odor, instead of every day. However, I don't recommend this technique for every dog, especially those who might bite down or struggle and hurt themselves, their owner, or both. But if you're sure your dog is mellow and trusting enough to safely try this, it's great fun, especially showing off to friends and relatives.

Donna Fritz

Arthur Finds A Short-Tailed Shrew

The recent thaw turned the yard from crisp white to mushy green and brown overnight. As welcome as the warmer temperatures were, when I bent to wipe my Golden Retriever's fuzzy feet after a vigorous session of frisbee, it was immediately obvious that the time had come for me to trim the fur between his toes again.

That I don't clip his feet neat until forced to do so by sloppy weather is due to a combination of personal aesthetics (I like the "Dr. Seuss feet" look) and sheer slothfulness. It's not Arthur's fault; he thoroughly enjoys the procedure, which includes tummy rubs, praise and petting.

Arthur's reward and the true test of a trim is to take him outside. This time it was also a test of my ability to identify what Arthur found in the driveway and proudly brought over to me. Now what? Rather than hurt his feelings, I held my hand palm up, and Arthur spit out a warm, sodden and pathetically tiny body into my pretty pink mitten. Great, a dead mouse.

"Good puppy." I smiled and patted him, pretending I appreciated his gift instead of being honest and flinging it into the woods. Then I inspected it with genuine interest and curiosity. This was no mouse, nor did it have the large, distinctive front feet of a mole.

I decided it must be a shrew. You can tell a shrew from a mouse by the shrew's much smaller eyes, and if you look closely, you can see that shrews have five toes, while mice have only four. If you care to take a really close look, instead of the wide, yellow, chisel-type incisors of a rodent, shrews have dark brown, pointy teeth suitable for crunching up insects, worms, snails, and occasionally salamanders, in addition to nuts and seeds.

There are several shrews native to New York State, including some interesting characters: the Smoky Shrew, which is grayish-brown in summer and, as its name suggests, smoky-gray in winter; the Masked Shrew, which is a grizzled brown on top, pale beneath, and in spite of its name, has no masklike marking of any kind; the Pygmy Shrew, the smallest mammal in the Americas; the Least Shrew, which will enter beehives to feast on larva, and a Water Shrew, which can run short distances on the surface of water.

What Arthur had brought me was a Northern Short-Tailed Shrew, a common but rarely-seen neighbor which lives in grass-lined burrows beneath rocks, logs, buildings and gardens. This particular species is large for a shrew, measuring up to four inches, including a tail less than one inch long. When not soaked in viscous dog spit, their fur is pearl-gray all over, thick and velvety soft with a beautiful silken luster. This gorgeous coat is not a luxury, but a vital necessity during our cold winter months. Shrews don't hibernate, and because they have a very high metabolism, they must eat every few hours or starve. They hunt and forage both day and night.

Shrews make a variety of sounds, including chirps and squeaks, and clicks during courtship, most of it barely audible to humans. In addition, they are believed to use echolocation, as bats do, to explore and find food. They tunnel through leaf litter, long grass and snow, which is probably where one of the local cats had found and killed this one, then walked away from the corpse in distaste. Shrews can secrete a foul-smelling musk to deter predators, but to me, this one smelled only of damp leaves and Arthur's chronic doggy breath.

The Northern Short-Tailed Shrew is the most fascinating of all our shrews. According to Cornell, they are one of the world's very few venomous mammals. Glands in this shrew's mouth produce a toxin that helps them subdue small birds and mammals, causing "irregular respiration, paralysis, and convulsions." Fortunately for Arthur and myself, shrews are nowhere near large enough to pose any sort of threat to even housecats, which in a suburban environment are one of their prime predators. Shrews are also killed and eaten by hawks, owls, foxes, snakes, raccooons, weasels, and skunks.

To make up for all this, shrews have an average of six babies per litter several times a year, but wild shrews are lucky to see their first birthday. Wherever this one had originally come from, I hoped there were more of these nifty little creatures, and that they would live out their lives unharmed. I buried the shrew beneath a rotted log, then took Arthur inside. It was time to brush his teeth again.

Lack of Exercise Turns Arthur into a Thieving Retriever

This cold weather is really hard on my soon-to-be six-year-old Golden Retriever (appropriately, Arthur's birthday is Valentine's Day.) No, he doesn't shiver in that luxurious golden coat, nor do his feet go numb; no, Arthur's problem with winter is much more difficult to fix, because it's me.

In the summer, it's one of life's simple pleasures to come home after work and throw a tennis ball or fabric frisbee until this energetic dog in the prime of life finally flops over, exhausted and content. It stays light out until eight or later, and jeans and a T-shirt are more than sufficient. But now it's dark by the time I get home, bitterly cold, and usually snowing; I get hypothermic long before Arthur even begins to get tired. I can't throw very far on a sunny day in July; when it's pitch black with flurries and I can't feel my fingers, I'm downright terrible. Arthur leans over to pick the toy up from the drift in front of us, spits it out on my frozen feet, then rolls in the snow, snorting a doggy laugh.

Walks on winter weekday nights are out of the question, and no matter how much I play with him on Saturday and Sunday, come Monday he's ready for more. He sleeps all day while I'm at work, and by evening is eager for attention and exercise, just when I'm ready to collapse.

(One quick note: Despite how he seems impervious to single-digit temperatures, given his druthers, Arthur prefers to sleep warm on the bed.)

So while I'm making dinner for me and the critters, Arthur pads around cheerfully, thwacking his tail off the cat's face, casting about for something portable with which to entertain himself. This pretty much means anything that weighs less than he does, and he continues this behavior well into the wee hours, turning him into a canine compulsive kleptomaniac.

He collects all these items on the so-called doggy bed, but there's no room for him to sleep there, due to the eclectic assortment of items purloined from various locations throughout the house, including, but not limited to: my umbrella, taken from the chair seat under the kitchen table; one elderly sock of indeterminate age and origin; a jar of peanut butter, unopened, taken from the counter (another of my bright ideas was teaching him to retrieve things from the counter); my new Preston and

Child hardcover novel (thankfully, with my bookmark still in place); a plastic shopping bag containing several packets of instant rice mix I had set aside for charity, on top of the kitchen table; my CAMERA (!) from inside my purse, miraculously unscathed; and the precious gold scarf I recently knitted up using yarn spun from the shedded fur of Arthur's uncle, Hobbes. The list goes on.

This morning I had to sort through a puppy pawnshop of stolen goods for my mittens (he had taken both), but his happy spirit when he came wagging over to help melted my annoyance, and I smooched his head and told him I loved him.

Arthur Meets a Northern Harrier

The other day, the weather was so nice that I took Arthur up to a rural hilltop on a mission to spy on wildlife, one of Arthur's favorite hobbies. The breeze was surprisingly brisk, but the temperature was warm enough that it was pleasant, even if it made my eyes sting to look directly into the wind. After only a few minutes, sure enough, we noticed a hawk hunting in the field across the street.

Well, I noticed the bird, anyway. Intent on the pungent organic fertilizer recently applied to the hayfield, Arthur seemed unaware of the majestic feathered predator not twenty feet above us. When I saw Arthur stop and drop his head low, I quickly called him to heel and crossed the deserted street, while he was still gold and not brown. He had just had a bath the previous evening, and I wanted to see if he could stay smelling nice for an entire twenty-four hours.

Distracted by my hand petting his silky head, he happily accompanied me, eyes squinting into the wind, tongue lolling, and one ear blown inside-out. Even prevented from rolling in manure, Arthur was having a blast. So was I, mesmerized by the sight of the magnificent hawk hunting unperturbed by our presence.

At first glance I had assumed it was a Red-Tailed hawk, but as we got closer I could see that the tail was held straight and narrow, not flared into a fan as Red-Tails do. Also, while its brown and white plumage looked similar to a juvenile Red-Tail, this hawk was slender and graceful where Red-Tails are stocky and powerful. Finally, its behavior was all wrong; instead of soaring in circles high on a thermal, this hawk systematically covered the field low and slow, occasionally pausing to hover in place against the howling wind.

She was a Northern Harrier, utterly wild and beautiful. Harriers, also known as Marsh Hawks, are unusual among raptors by their obvious color differences between male and female. Males are mostly pale gray, while females are brown and white. Both have a distinctive white rump.

Harriers differ from other hawks in some fascinating ways. They have the same keen eyesight as other raptors, but also hunt using their acute hearing. Their face looks like an owl's and for the same reason: their round arrangement of stiff feathers helps catch the tiniest sounds of mice, voles and other small rodents. They have been documented drowning prey that would otherwise be too large for them to kill. Depending on the food supply, one male will often pair up with two or more females at the same time, and surprisingly, he's no deadbeat dad -- the male Harrier provides most of the food for his families. Females incubate the eggs and then care for the young in a nest of vegetation on the ground.

Arthur simply ignored the magnificent bird overhead, hot on the scent of something or other, snuffling around in the damp earth. I was paying way too much attention to the hawk and not enough to my dog. I glanced at Arthur to see him execute his patented stop, drop and roll. When he came up he had acquired a generous muddy streak from shoulders to hips, and sported one quizzical brown eyebrow. He'd stayed clean almost eighteen hours -- not a full day, but still a record.

Donna Fritz

Arthur and the Mystery of the Vanishing Lacrosse Ball

In the never-ending search for increasingly robust workouts for my eighty-pound golden retriever that don't include a heart attack for his human, I found his old orange lacrosse ball, and a hockey stick. Taking it on faith that there are neither Lacrosse Police nor Hockey Police to object, I called Arthur over, then used the hockey stick to sharply smack the orange ball, flinging it across the yard with an untalented but effective swing.

Unfortunately, Arthur missed the process entirely. For him, one second the ball was there; the next it was gone. He looked about, then started sniffing in the immediate area as if I'd hidden the ball.

"Out there," I said, pointing to where the orange ball sat on the hillside, plainly visible against the newly-mown lawn. Of course, to a dog the orange/green contrast might not be as obvious, but he understood the command and hand signal, and galloped off in the general direction, casting about in wide arcs until he stumbled across the toy.

Back he came with his usual headlong locomotive sprint, complete with trainlike sound as he huffed air in and out of his deep chest. Veering aside at the last possible second before running me down, he trotted back and spit out the ball -- literally; the ball was now covered with a layer of doggy drool -- and laid down with it in front of him.

Ah, but this time I didn't have to handle the slobbery thing! Instead I used the hockey stick to work the slimy lacrosse ball deftly out from between Arthur's forepaws, while Arthur looked on, rather perplexed at this novel manner in which I took the retrieved item from him.

Tapping the ball with the hockey stick to draw the dog's attention to it, I once again sent the lacrosse ball over a dozen yards away in the blink of an eye. Once again, Arthur stared in astonishment at the place the ball had been. Amazing! It had vanished! Wagging at this nifty mystery, Arthur stood and started circling, trying to pick up a scent trail to follow.

Hadn't he heard the heavy, solid-rubber ball thunk down onto the turf? If even my human ears could detect it, surely Arthur's keener sense of hearing did as well. Nope, not a clue. I had to send him out by voice and gesture again.

This time when he brought it back, I made him sit-stay several feet from the ball as I stepped up with the hockey stick, giving Arthur a chance to watch from a bit further away, in hopes of him seeing the stick hit the ball and the ball go through the air to land on the ground, not just the ball magically disappearing.

It took several tries before my dear, myopic dog finally, finally! grasped what was happening, and raced off the instant the lacrosse ball shot out across the yard. Triumphantly he returned with it clenched between his teeth, his whole body wagging hard, his eyes squinty and ears laid back with pleasure.

After that it was just a matter of repetition, until Arthur finally declared exhaustion by dropping to the ground, panting too hard to hold onto the orange ball. When he started ripping up the lawn as he often does,

I cringed and yelled at him to stop and come -- but I wasn't wincing at the divots. I was grossed out by a particularly disgusting TV show I'd seen, which included fascinatingly repulsive videos of various parasites which lurk in innocent-looking grass and leaves.

I'm talking about nastier things than even ticks: roundworms, tapeworms and heartworms. At least ticks you can see and pull off.

One of the most disgusting displays of rude disregard for health and safety is when someone walking their dog on one of those fifteen-foot retractable leashes stands nonchalantly by the road as their dog leaves a present on someone else's lawn. Who knows the last time they wormed that dog? If ever? Weeks later, even through rain, those eggs, larvae, worms and cysts are lurking in the environment, waiting for my beautiful Arthur to pick up in his mouth a ball that rolled through that mess.

Nor is Arthur the only one in danger; if a kid picks up that ball and then eats an ice cream cone without washing his hands, those canine-specific worms find themselves in the wrong host, but attempt to finish their life cycle anyway, with potentially horrific results for the child -- not only severe illness, but possibly blindness and even death. Please pick up after your dog!

Fortunately there's a simple way to keep your dog safely parasite-free: first you should take your chum to the vet, to make sure he isn't in danger of a deadly blockage if you suddenly kill all the worms in his arteries, heart or intestines; then give him regular doses of wormer as directed. Too bad we can't safeguard children as easily.

Arthur Goes Swimming in Little York Lake

On Sunday, several unusual events finally came together: the weather was nice, I felt alert and ready for action, and it wasn't a workday. Arthur, like most dogs, is always ready for adventure. Go ahead, ask your dog if he wants to play at three AM. Chances are he'd be delighted.

When my Golden Retriever saw me pull out the denim bag I use for his stuff, he grabbed one of his scruffy Sesame Street dolls and wagged over to me.

"I don't think Ernie can swim," I informed Arthur. To be honest, Ernie sometimes gives me the creeps, peering out at us from under the furniture -- but Arthur loves the thing, so I've never quite had the heart to mail it off to Saskatchewan with no return address, as I'd like to.

"Here," I said, to distract him from it. "How about this?" With a flourish I produced one of our professional training dummies, and Arthur spit out Ernie like last week's leftovers to grab the proffered toy. A training dummy always means an extra fun time.

As I gathered up my camera, towels, a brush and other such sundries, Arthur carried the dummy around in aimless excited circles, his happy tail thwacking the cat across the face. Accustomed to such indignities, Sly didn't take offense, but I noticed he decided to continue his feline supervision from the top of the dryer.

Arthur carried the dummy out to the car, helping by not trying to help do anything else, and we were off.

It was still early in the evening on a beautiful lake, but we were nearly alone. One kid was fishing from the footbridge, and two people in kayaks paddled leisurely out on the water. Perfect.

When I opened the door, Arthur exploded out, still carrying the white rubber training dummy. I got my camera and a towel, and we sauntered over the footbridge and strolled downstream to where the water was deep enough for an eighty-pound dog to swim. Well, I sauntered and strolled; Arthur twitched, panted, wagged and tossed his head, but he held himself strictly in check and remained by my side with nothing controlling him but his own strength of will.

"Good puppy," I approved, patting his head when we arrived at a nice shelving bank. I held my hand out for the toy in his mouth, and Arthur immediately dropped it, then shoved his wet snout into my hand. I petted him, but of course that didn't calm him down, so I gave up and gently tossed the toy into the water by its rope handle.

"Okay," I said, releasing him as if from a catapult (dog-apult?)

But, as Arthur could tell you (although he's too well-mannered to do so) I'm a terrible toy thrower. The nubbly dummy landed about ten feet from shore, but the current quickly washed it right up to the bank. Arthur reached down and picked the toy up, barely getting his front feet wet. Clearly disappointed, he brought it back to me and dropped it at my feet, inviting me to try again.

This time I swung the dummy up and out, and it plopped down in the middle of the stream.

"Okay," I told him, and off like a shot he went, splashing ecstatically out until only his head and powerful shoulders were above the water. He bore down on the moving toy, grabbed it in his jaws, then turned and headed back, self-satisfaction shining in his eyes.

As if being timed, he raced back to me and dropped the toy.

"Excel--" I began, just as Arthur shook his wet self vigorously. At the very last second I twisted the camera behind my body before it got drenched in lake water. From twenty feet away, the water appeared crystalline clear; up close and personal, it smelled suspiciously of dead snails. "--AAAAUUGHH!" I finished, but I was laughing, and Arthur loves when I laugh.

"Stay," I admonished, and hiked back to the car to put the camera in a much safer place. Only the case had gotten wet, so I considered myself lucky.

When I came back, he hadn't moved, so I praised him into idiocy and threw the toy into the water several more times. Then we played fetch on dry land until Arthur's coat was almost back to fluffy again.

Even dry, Arthur smelled vaguely of dead aquatic organisms, so I gave him a few quick swipes along his sides and back with a fresh dryer sheet, and he's tolerable until I can give him a bath. For me, a shower and fresh pajamas did the trick, but my sneakers are banished to the front stoop until they can be thrown in the washer.

Cooler Weather Makes Perfect Time to Play

It was a delight and relief to play with my Golden Retriever on the lawn yesterday during daylight hours. Everything was perfect: the lawn had been mowed two days earlier, so neither Arthur nor myself would get grass stains (OK, some, but not a lot), and the weather had finally relented, the oven-like temperatures giving way to a pleasantly cool afternoon with a nice breeze.

I got right down on my knees, and Arthur danced around wild with joy, looking as always for something to retrieve. The only thing he could find that smelled like me was, well, me. He closed his jaws around my sweatshirt sleeve and did some fancy footwork. I suspect he was trying to bring it to me ... he's sweet and gentle, devoted and absolutely gorgeous -- but he doesn't always think things through. I just laughed and twisted my arm in the soaking-wet sleeve so I could shove him away with both hands.

This of course is the invitation to play hard. When he was a tiny puppy, I would set a toy behind me and then lightly shove him bodily, sparking the natural urge to roughhouse that nearly every dog has. Arthur weighs 80 pounds now, and pound-for-pound dogs are much stronger than humans, but the only real pain he inflicted was when I huddled in a ball so he couldn't reach my sleeve, and in his frenzy of snuffling and pushing his nose beneath my neck and shoulders, he stepped on my hair. Ow.

I was soon physically tired from this exuberant play, and lay on my back on the lawn, catching my breath. The grass still had a touch of that wonderful, childhood-evoking fresh-cut scent, the sky was blue with a few puffy white clouds, and there was a crisp breeze. I seriously considered going inside for a blanket and taking a nice nap outside, but closed my eyes instead. It would be too much effort to get up.

Meanwhile, Arthur was barely warmed up. He ran idiot circles around my somnolent form, dashing in to thrust his cold wet nose in my face every few laps. Spurred by an impulse which I immediately regretted, I suddenly reached up and squeezed his black nose, saying "BEEP!"

He instantly went berserk, jumping on top of me and grabbing my sodden sleeve again, but this time in his enthusiasm he happened to catch a pinch of skin. I stifled the yelp of surprise and pain. He was having such fun, and after all I *had* beeped his nose. He just had way more energy than I did.

I stood up, wondering if I should whip up a bowl of Cream of Iams soup for myself, since apparently my previous night's fudgesicle dinner wasn't doing the trick. Pulling the fabric frisbee from the corner on the porch, I threw the ratty-looking but beloved thing until Arthur eventually declared he'd had enough by running past me to the door. Either he was tired or thirsty, or both. It was good to see him tired and happy.

It's cool enough that we didn't have the windows open last night, so I don't know if our weird nocturnal bird is still out there. It was very strange to hear a low, clear wolf-whistle in the dark, coming from behind our neighbor's house at three AM. It might have been some sort of stalker, except Arthur ignored it entirely, and it takes a seriously devoted stalker to whistle appreciatively every few minutes for over two hours. And yes, it was impossible to sleep with that going on, and too hot to shut the windows that night. (Later I decided it must be a

Chuck-Will's-Widow, an insect-eating night bird, unusual this far north.)

There is an up side to the hot weather. Arthur can only enjoy playing hard after the sun has gone down, and chasing a frisbee by the wan porch light is less about agility and speed than honing his finding skills. It's no longer an easy run-and-catch, sometimes he loses track of where it is and has to hunt around for a minute or so. One night I took advantage of this delay to snap some pictures of him.

Later, when sharing the pictures with friends, I smiled to see how happy my beautiful chum is, and the spring in his step at nine years plus. Too bad the photos also mercilessly showed every detail of the grimy toy this gorgeous show-quality dog is carrying. I'll get him a new Flippy Flopper this weekend.

Arthur Observes a Garter Snake Catch-and-Release Project

Like all dogs, my Golden Retriever occasionally needs a bath. One of the up sides to all this hot weather is that I can just use the well water straight from the hose, and not bother dragging gallon jugs of warm water outside as I have to do in the colder weather. (Anyone who suggests that you bathe a long-haired, thickly-furred dog inside is either a plumber, related to one, or has stock in Dran-O.)

Another plus is that Arthur loves baths. I'm not sure if it's the pleasure of a full-body massage, the cooling effect of getting sopping wet on a hot day, or my undivided attention and constant praise. Probably all three. Also like most dogs, Arthur pays very close attention to what I am doing, and has learned that when I gather up shampoo and towels and head outside, it's Bath Time. He went nuts.

After the initial frenzy (even at nine years old, Arthur does nothing halfheartedly) he went to pee at the edge of the woods, then galumphed back toward me where I was setting the shampoo down and turning the hose on. Anyone who has read Lewis Carroll's *The Jabberwocky* and wondered what "galumphing" is, it's a kind of gleeful gallop with more enthusiasm than grace.

Suddenly I yelled without looking back at him: "Arthur! STAY!!" There was a big green-and-yellow garter snake laying peacefully unsuspecting, hidden beautifully in among the coils of the green hose. I've seen and tried unsuccessfully to catch this snake many times; he seems to live beneath the wooden stoop of the front porch. Over a dozen failures only served to whet my desire to get hold of him. Not to remove him, because he eats bugs and mice; and certainly not to kill him, but merely because I have never matured enough to be satisfied enjoying wildlife from a distance. I wanted to hold him, just for a minute.

I cannot stress this enough: It is *always* a bad idea to grab wild animals. Don't do it.

The lengthwise yellow stripes on the olive-drab body were reasonably convincing that this was, indeed, a garter snake, who has no lethal defense against humans. (We do have rattlesnakes around here.) I lunged, and to my vast surprise, I caught him!

Arthur, watching from his ten-foot exile, must have decided to temper my command with his own judgment, because I felt a warm furry presence at my back. In the pleasure of finally getting hold of our elusive resident reptile, I didn't rebuke him. Besides, I was a little preoccupied.

The snake objected to the perceived attack with teeth and musk glands. I had miscalculated enough that he had sufficient leeway to whip his head around and sink his inward-pointing, razor-sharp teeth into the soft inside of my wrist. Garter snakes are not venomous, but something in his saliva made me bleed way more than the simple physical injury would account for.

But biting wasn't the worst of it. Oh, no. This guy was so panicky that he lashed his tail back and forth, spraying and wiping a hideous-smelling musk from his anal glands all over me in a truly horrible form of biological warfare. Ugh.

Still, it was ineffective, and he got tired and gave up. I pried his face off my arm, got a more comfortable grip (for me) and rinsed him and my arms off as best I could with the hose. Then I went inside, snake, dog, and all. I urgently needed to change my shirt, and wanted my camera.

Only when I got back outside and really inspected my prize did I discover why I was able to catch this guy. I hadn't gotten faster or more clever. He was about to shed, and the scales over his eyes were a milky blue. He was temporarily half-blind. In addition, in my amateur opinion, the snake's slender tail indicated "he" is probably a she.

I took several photos, then gently set the snake back down by the hose where I'd gotten her. It took her a second or two to realize she was free, then she sinuously melted into the grass like quicksilver.

Well, I couldn't give Arthur a bath now; I didn't want to terrify the snake any further. I picked everything up and we went back inside, to Arthur's obvious disappointment. A biscuit temporarily mollified him, but I could tell he had been looking forward to that bath.

Later that evening, when the temperature had cooled down and the snake had had plenty of time to go back to her normal snake agenda, I took Arthur out for some frisbee fun, and he finally completely forgave me. Another biscuit afterwards didn't hurt.

(*Days later the bite marks were still swollen and very red. I think I'll leave even garter snakes alone from now on.*)

Arthur Helps With the Gardening

Like most companion dogs, my golden retriever Arthur loves to help with whatever I'm doing. His motto is, "It doesn't matter what we do, as long as we're together." He's especially enthusiastic about any project that involves going outside, from filling the birdfeeders to landscaping projects.

On the principle that more flowers equals less mowing, I'm continually adding perennials as time and finances permit. Annuals defy the concept of "Do something right and you don't have to do it again." Although many annuals are beautiful, I prefer investing in plants that will dutifully show up year after year with minimal fuss beyond basic weeding and watering.

Perennials have the added bonus of being fairly cheap after the initial spring planting frenzy has passed. Often the leftovers sell for a dollar apiece or less, if you don't mind waiting -- or if you're like me, and only get around to it long after the recommended planting season. I have a patch of lily-of-the-valley that smells just as delightful as if I'd paid full price -- maybe even more so.

Another factor I like to consider is whether it's going to help out the local wildlife, bringing critters in close where I can enjoy watching them. A friend with an invasion of butterfly bush and a trumpet vine (which has pretty much swallowed her entire front porch) has a dozen or more of jewel-like hummingbirds flitting about, with their signature magical hum. Next year I'll get cuttings and add those plants to my yard.

I also have the old standby herbs: sage, thyme, oregano, winter savory and lavender. These tend to take over in a way that leaves little foothold for weeds. What I like best about them is not their small, short-lived flowers, but their resilience. These even survive the regular "waterings" Arthur thoughtfully bestows on them when I'm not paying enough attention. (And now you know the reason why I only use storebought herbs to cook with.)

Recently it became obvious that Arthur isn't the only one to help with my landscaping efforts. Several cheerful sunflowers have added their bright yellow faces to the front garden, presumably planted by the industrious squirrels who bury things for safekeeping. I doubt any seeds could have just lain there unnoticed long enough to germinate, with all the mourning doves that creep around under the plants scratching mulch out of the garden and onto the lawn, in their never-ending quest for anything edible.

So there I was with a trowel, a jug of water, several pots of plants, and of course Arthur. Combining dirt, water, and a retriever is a great idea, if you ask the retriever. Ask the person who has to clean the floor later and they'll probably disagree. Ah well, it's summer. He'll dry off before we go back inside, I told myself.

Arthur loves to roll, especially on freshly-mown grass. I mentally shrugged and let him have fun. He wiggled and writhed belly-side-up with pure canine enjoyment while I put in the new flowers and did some light weeding. I finished up by watering the newcomers, then said, "Hey Arth."

Instantly Arthur stood, wagging and panting happily. The whole left side of his face was streaked artfully with bright chlorophyll green. He sneezed, shook himself, then looked me right in the eye and rolled onto and over the tender new hosta I had just carefully planted.

Although I'd never say it out loud to my chum, sometimes my motto is, "If it gets any worse, I'll have to ask you to stop helping me." Luckily for Arthur, he's worth more than any plant. Besides, aren't hostas supposed to be tough?

I kissed the one small unstained area on top of his head, shook the last remaining drops of the water onto the sad-looking plant by way of apology, then let Arthur carry the empty jug back. Halfway to the house, he dropped it, missed the handle, and grabbed it by the corner, crunching down solidly to meet this challenge.

He's worth more than an empty milk jug, too.

Milkweed in the Garden

Early Saturday morning, before the heat grew oppressive, I took Arthur for a walk down the seasonal road. Everything is blooming, the cicadas are buzzing, and the birds are out looking for food to fill their babies' bellies. Nature is running rampant.

There were hardly any mosquitoes, even down by the swamp. I stopped to look at and take pictures of a buttonbush with its round white fuzzball flowers, and Arthur took advantage of my momentary lapse in vigilance to roll in the mud at the edge of the road. Barely ten minutes in, and already he sported a coat that was partly his customary fine-spun gold, and part brown smears that smelled suspiciously of dead snails. Yay for Nature.

I admired some swamp milkweed, a taller and showier version of the more familiar Common Milkweed, which I have growing in front of my garden.

My appreciation of the local plants and insects was rudely cut short as I abruptly realized that while the mosquitoes might be temporarily quiescent, the deerflies were very much alert and active -- and bloodthirsty. Our walk back quickly turned into a light jog, to Arthur's undisguised delight. I doubt he even knew the carnivorous insects were there, protected as he is by his luxurious woven coat; but man, I sure did. We beat a hasty retreat back home, where I continued photographing flowers.

The lone milkweed in my garden volunteered there and I allowed it to remain, although I remove grass and other uninvited interlopers. Leaving milkweed to grow unchecked amongst the tomatoes and strawberries sounds like an insane thing to do -- after all, it's a "weed," isn't it?

Well, no. First of all, Common Milkweed (Asclepias syriaca) is considered edible by those who enjoy foraging. I've eaten the tender new leaves served boiled, like spinach -- although mostly because I was a guest, everyone else at the table seemed to regard it as regular fare, and I didn't want to appear impolite. It was mildly bitter, but not bad with butter and salt, and did me no harm.

But more importantly, the gorgeous Monarch butterfly relies exclusively on milkweed leaves for food as a caterpillar, and uses the nectar of the flowering plant to fuel its astounding migration. Loss of wild spaces due to increased demand for housing and businesses has meant loss of milkweed, with devastating consequences for this beautiful butterfly.

However, individual homeowners can make a difference simply by planting native wildflowers instead of mowing acres of sterile lawn, saving themselves the expense and hassle of maintaining an unnatural yard, plus providing food and shelter for many different species. Even a small, out-of-the-way area can be a butterfly haven, and native plants often thrive in places where fancy foreign cultivars refuse to survive.

My friend Cindi has taken this concept to a level most of us can only stare at, wide-eyed in amazement. Her backyard would be an inspiration on the cover of any gardening magazine, with its myriad carefully-planned and well-tended specimens artfully arranged along graceful, twisted paths, complete with a pergola festooned with flowering vines. There's even a fishpond.

But even a more modest effort can make a difference to hungry winged travelers, and besides milkweed flowers (which grow in clusters referred to as "umbels") smell heavenly.

At home, I wandered over to my little milkweed, who stood tall and straight next to the tumbled tomato vines. It still hasn't flowered, but it's in the shade of a big droopy pine tree.

Peering closer, I noticed a bunch of tiny insects in the crease of a few of the milkweed leaves, and a couple of rather large black ants, who seemed to be … keeping watch over the little bugs? One ant actually ran toward my camera lens in an aggressive bluff when I got too close. Ants don't eat milkweed. In fact, very few insects have evolved a tolerance for the toxins in milkweed sap. So what were they doing there?

I took some pictures and when enlarged, the small critters proved to be aphids -- with ants "tending" them. I had heard somewhere of ants milking aphids for the sweet honeydew they produce, even protecting their aphid "herd" from other insects, but had never seen it myself before.

My excitement must have been obvious to my canine companion, for Arthur came over to see what it was that I found so fascinating. Before I could intervene, he sneezed violently onto the aphids and ants alike, but they seemed unfazed.

Apparently dog snot is something else they've evolved to survive.

I laughed and thumped his furry sides in amusement, which turned him into a complete lunatic. Chasing circles on the front lawn, he snatched up his fabric frisbee and carried it over to me in an entreaty he knew I'd be helpless to resist.

He's a good puppy.

Fall Leaf Raking with a Vulture

Saturday was one of those picture-perfect autumn days, with a blue sky and crisp air spiced with the tang of fallen leaves. I frowned as my companion Arthur -- a burnished-gold vision of youthful strength and silken fur, scion of a long line of red-letter Golden Retriever champions -- rolled onto his back in the dead leaves, all four feet waving in the air, a yard-long branch clenched in his mouth.

"Arthur," I reproved vaguely.

Delighted at the prospect of attention, Arthur scrambled to get his feet beneath him and padded over to me, brandishing the hunk of wood, maple leaves clinging to his coat.

"Yeah, yeah, I know," I said with a sigh. "There's more leaves here than you can shake a stick at."

Really, they needed to be raked up before the snow came and mashed them flat against the grass, killing it.

"Wanna help?" I asked Arthur. Silly question.

I headed for the shed, to fetch up the rake and the old sheet kept just for this purpose. Still with the piece of maple tree held horizontally in his jaws, Arthur would have followed -- or attempted to, anyhow.

"Arth," I said, before he got jolted by the branch catching in the doorway. Reluctantly he spit out the branch and the pieces of wet bark, then he stood, waiting for me to allow him in, rather like a vampire who cannot cross the threshold uninvited.

This is a useful bit of training, if your dog is over ten pounds and you ever have snow, rain, mud, grass clippings or anything in your yard that you don't want tracked inside onto your delft-blue oriental carpet. As always, the key here is consistency: it can be as simple as making him wait for your okay every time he comes in, or more specifically, just when you say something, as Arthur does. This time it took me by surprise for a moment; I didn't remember the rule that he had to wait until I said he could come in, after I spoke to him at the door -- but Arthur remembered, and obeyed.

Never underestimate the ability of a dog to differentiate between situations, either. The simple syllable "Arth" means very different things under different circumstances. Outside it means "come here now." Inside, depending on my tone, it can mean "come here" or "stop doing that" (pestering the cat, licking his paws, or almost anything annoying.) In the doorway it means, variously, "let the cat in first" or "wait until I wipe your feet off and invite you in."

This time Arthur waited politely until I said, "Okay," then he launched himself into the shed. Rarely does Arthur walk sedately of his own free will, and my purposeful manner let him know something was up, and made him eager to help. (Although I often suspect his motto is, "If I'm not in the way, I can move.")

I did, in fact, have something he could do that could technically be termed useful, or at least didn't qualify as a hindrance. I found the rake, leaned it by the door, then got out the old sheet and held it for Arthur to take.

"Bring it out with us," I told him.

Ecstatic at being included in the fun, Arthur seized the duck-print sheet between his teeth and wagged hard, sneezing but not letting go of the dusty cloth.

Picking up the rake on my way out, I held the door for Arthur, who proudly trailed his sheet behind him like some sort of demented bride, tripping clumsily on it as he went.

Somehow he managed to wrestle the bedsheet all the way to the front lawn, where I suddenly realized that letting him play with it was probably not a good idea. You can't hand a dog something, then yell at him for grabbing it later, like when it's full of leaves. With this premonition in mind, I ordered Arthur to go lay down for the duration.

Raking was a pleasantly monotonous task, punctuated only by filling the sheet and dragging it to the leaf pile (no, I didn't let Arthur help with this part of the project, although he enthusiastically volunteered.) Eventually most of the worst of the leaves were consigned to the pile, and I indulged myself and my furry friend by cuddling with him on the leafy-smelling sheet, gazing idly up at the crystal-blue sky.

A lone turkey vulture circled far overhead, its silhouette identifiable by the strong dihedral (V-shape) formed by its wings as it rode the thermal, looking and sniffing for dinner. Turkey vultures are one of the few birds with any sense of smell at all, which is why it's OK to put a baby bird back in the nest; the mother can't smell your scent. Vultures depend upon their keen sense of smell to locate dead and decaying animals. They're part of Nature's cleanup crew.

This vulture apparently didn't find anything in our vicinity, for it wheeled out of sight behind the trees just as the sun started to disappear as well, and I noticed it was starting to get chilly.

"Come on, Arthur," I said, standing and ruffling his fur. "Can you bring the sheet back in?"

Bring was already in his vocabulary, and he had recently enjoyed carrying the old sheet. Arthur guessed correctly and pounced on the sheet, wagging madly when I praised him.

"EXcellent!" I said, driving all rational thought from his brain. Gleefully Arthur half-dragged, half-fought the sheet all the way to the shed, and I let him savor the satisfaction of accomplishing the difficult task on his own.

Arthur's Christmas Fun at Lucille's

As early as seven a.m., my fuzzy gold dog knew something was up. It was Friday, and our usual day to go to Lucille's is Sunday, not that dogs can tell which day of the week it is -- or can they? Maybe it was the pet crate sitting by the front door (not for him; my beloved little eleven-pound Sonia often accompanies us when we visit friends.)

Whatever the clue, Arthur knew something special was on the agenda. Eagerly he cast about for one of the ubiquitous stuffed animals in varying stages of disrepute that litter the floor. Finding a relatively intact teddy bear, he grabbed it, sneezing as the plush fur folded over his wet black nose, but not letting go. Carrying things isn't so much a deliberate decision on his part as it's like software pre-loaded on your computer. Sure, with a lot of hard work and know-how, you could change it, but wouldn't it be easier to just make sure you get what you want in the first place?

That's one of the best things about purebred dogs: you can fairly accurately predict their personalities and habits. Retrievers as a group like to carry things; that's just a fact. Golden Retrievers in particular are also famous for their mellow nature. Aggression simply isn't part of their skill set, so if you want a guard dog, look elsewhere. Further, each genetic line shows distinctive traits which that breeder specifically chose to enhance.

For generation upon generation, Goldens were selectively bred for their desire to retrieve, as well as gentleness, intelligence, and beauty. Despite their eagerness to please and powerful build, Arthur's line is not a serious hunter's dog, to crash through bracken and wade through swampland -- not because any of the dogs in Arthur's clan would be reluctant to do these things and more, but because their gorgeous show-ring coat is a burdock magnet and mud sponge.

Fortunately, the temperature didn't go high enough for mud until after our holiday socializing. Nothing says "Merry Christmas" quite like a kitchen floor full of muddy paw-prints. It helps to keep the fur between Arthur's toes trimmed, but that just means he leaves neater, more easily-identified incriminating evidence.

With presents, pets, and lots of seasonal cheer, we got in the car to go to Lucille's to celebrate Christmas a day late.

"Arthur, you wanna go see Lucille?" I asked over my shoulder.

Excited whines filled the car. Arthur knows Lucille's name.

My dear friend is an accomplished chef, and the delicious aroma of roast beef greeted us at the door, thoroughly justifying Arthur's delighted enthusiasm. Immediately upon entering, he dived for the stuffed toys kept in the corner for him (a retriever's answer to any happy situation is to carry something) then he wagged over to Lucille for attention and petting, both of which she gladly gave. Larry, too, joined in, adding some dog biscuits from the box on the table. Arthur was ecstatic.

This seemed like as good a time as any to open presents. As usual, Arthur had more presents than anyone else, each bag of treats wrapped separately for maximum shredding enjoyment. And enjoy them he did, tossing scraps aside and ripping into his gifts, once even going through the thick foil packaging. What fun! I interrupted his revels only to feed him from the opened package, and tape one of the bows to the top of his silken head.

The final parcel contained a stuffed reindeer, which Lucille had thoughtfully purchased without a squeaker. Something new to carry! Arthur thumped the floor approvingly with his thick golden tail, mouthing his toy without harming it (spit doesn't count) in the way typical of most Goldens.

Arthur had had enough excitement that he lay still and well-behaved during the meal, knowing full well that Lucille and I would both feed him tidbits after (emphatically not during) our meal. I do try to regulate how much "people food" Arthur gets at Lucille's, and he isn't allowed any of the fatty trimmings.

According to one Cornell veterinarian, the days immediately following Thanksgiving and Christmas see the most pets brought in for "dietary indiscretion" -- in other words, people feed their animal chums large amounts of rich fatty foods they're not used to, resulting in upset stomach, vomiting, diarrhea, and even pancreatitis, which can be fatal.

The trick is to give your dog tiny pieces instead of big hunks. Arthur doesn't have time to gauge the size of a treat; he'll gulp down an entire burger as quickly as a shred the size of a pencil eraser. He goes by smell, and has way more fun receiving a dozen smaller treats than one or two large ones, even though the total amount might be the same, or even less with the many little tidbits. It's fun, not food quantity, that matters most.

This evening I told him we're going back to Lucille's on New Year's Day. Don't try to tell me dogs don't understand what you say to them. He knew exactly what my words meant, and he's already looking forward to it.

Arthur Goes Hiking at Buttermilk Falls

On Memorial Day, I took Arthur to Buttermilk Falls. He sat and panted his excitement in locomotive huffs, so we drove through Ithaca with the windows down in the chill morning temperature for his comfort, not mine.

Once at the park, I let him out in the parking lot, led him to the weeds and encouraged him to do anything he might have to do. He'd gone before we left, but after getting all worked up during the trip, you never know – and while we do carry plastic bags (well, Arthur carries everything) in case of emergency on the trails, it's better to avoid the problem entirely if possible.

Arthur dilly-dallied around, sniffing and marking beneath the brambles and goldenrod edging the pavement. When he finished, he padded over and looked up at me for approval. (One drawback to training your dog to pee on command: every time thereafter, they expect to be praised for the act.)

Glancing down at his face, I frowned. He had a big dark eyeball booger on his nose. Yuck. I went to wipe it off, and instead gingerly picked it up on my finger, inspecting it more closely.

IT WAS A TICK.

It must've dropped down on him from the underbrush. Filthy, wicked things! I drove my thumbnail across its body, then flicked it onto the tarmac and scraped my sneaker over it, mooshing it into a smear of hemolymph (bug blood) – a deeply satisfying act of violence.

When it comes to parasites, I cheerfully employ chemical warfare, and Arthur is dosed religiously with one of the spot products from the vet which kills fleas and ticks, and also repels mosquitoes.

While I dislike both fleas and ticks on general principles, I truly loathe ticks on specifics of behavior as well. Several species of these noxious critters are common to our area, all active and ravenous from early Spring until the heavy frosts of Fall.

Ticks are not insects, but arthropods, distant cousins to spiders and lobsters. Ugly things, they all have biting/sucking/anchoring mouth parts which enable them to bury their entire head into the flesh of their unsuspecting victim, transmitting any diseases they've picked up along the way, as they drink your dog's blood (or yours) in preparation for molting or making more ticks. According to Cornell's website, the more blood a female tick drinks, the more eggs she can produce -- from a few hundred to several thousand eggs.

Adult ticks like to lurk on tall grasses, and wait until carbon dioxide, ammonia, and/or body heat cue them that a potential host is nearby. They do not jump or fly, but some will crawl up to 23 yards toward a victim.

Some of our most common varieties are two different dog ticks (these are the ones that swell up to a gray balloon), Lone Star ticks, groundhog ticks, and blacklegged ticks (also called deer ticks). They transmit several diseases in this area: Rocky Mountain Spotted Fever (can be fatal if not treated promptly), Lyme Disease (untreated, this may cause chronic joint, neurological or cardiac problems), Human Babesiosis (a malaria-like illness that can result in death.)

Trying to remove a tick with chemicals or matches might make the tick regurgitate its stomach contents, increasing the chance of disease. The recommended way to remove one is to get a grip on its head as close to the skin of the host as possible (tweezers are useful) and pull slowly until it lets go. Clean the area as you would a scratch, then I like to have some sort of ceremonial destruction of the tick. It gives me a sense of victory to drown it in alcohol.

Some disgusting tick factoids: there are over 800 known species of ticks; they can ingest 624 times their weight in blood in a single feeding; and one female tortoise tick laid over 23 thousand eggs in a single batch.

I've had to pull two of them off Arthur in his five years; fortunately, with the spot treatment from the vet, now any ticks that bite my beloved mutt die. We had an exhilarating walk along the Buttermilk Falls trails, although we kept it to about an hour in deference to my out-of-shape self. I was exhausted when we got home, but Arthur considered the hilly hike a mere warmup, and required a session with the Flippy Flopper to satisfy him. I've gotten pretty good at throwing it while laying flat on my back on the lawn. So much for exercising your dog to get you in shape!

Arthur Enjoys Our So-Called Spring

"Arthur," I called to my exuberant golden retriever. This cold weather is ideal for a dog wearing a thick fuzzy coat, giving him energy and zest. I just shivered, and tried to hunch farther into my coat and scarf. He ran wild circles around me, shoving his nose into the fresh snow, sneezing happily, while I hugged myself, tucking my mittened hands under my arms. Wasn't it supposed to be Spring?

About the only fun thing this morning was seeing that our cottontail rabbit neighbor had hopped across the backyard, halfway down the driveway, and across the front yard, where the tracks disappeared into the small stand of trees. Arthur paid no attention to the bunny prints. He's an excellent tracker when I ask him to find a person or item, but not much of a hunter, being both bred and trained to coexist peacefully with other animals.

So Arthur made doggy snow angels while I backtracked our long-eared visitor. Occasionally I toss overripe fruit out by the trees, in an attempt to help out beneficial wildlife such as opossums, without attracting the ones I'd prefer not to interact with, like raccoons and skunks. Bunnies like apples, even soft apples with brown spots, and this one had indeed been munching on the now-frozen apples.

Cottontail rabbits are one of the species that has benefited from humans cutting down the trees and cultivating short tender grass and other tasty crops. In fact, rabbits like our lawns so much that very soon, they will be using them as nurseries. Pulling fur from her own chest, momma rabbit will make a small nest, often smack in the middle of an open yard, and proceed to leave her offspring there for the entire day. This is normal.

Unlike adult cottontail rabbits, the babies have nearly no scent at all. If Mom were to keep them close to her, any predator drawn to her scent would find them. Without her, they stand a good chance of being overlooked by predators, most of which hunt by smell. The mother only needs to feed her babies briefly at dawn and again at dusk. They do not need her for warmth.

One of the banes of a wildlife rehabilitator's life is well-meaning folk bringing in "orphan" baby animals which are not orphans at all, but kidnapped from parents too timid to defend them. With all our fancy technology and heroic efforts, the best mother for a baby rabbit is still Momma Rabbit.

If you discover a litter of rabbit kits in your yard, the best thing to do is keep children and pets away from them. If you must relocate them (because they are in danger or the nest has been destroyed by a pet or lawnmower), rub your hands with grass to minimize your scent, then make a similar shallow form nearby. include some of the mother's fur from the original nest and then move the babies as gently as possible, handling them only as much as absolutely necessary. Your scent on them will NOT make their mother abandon them, but the stress of being handled can kill them. Leave the area quickly, and try to keep it as quiet as possible.

Rabbit babies are among the most delicate of wild critters. They may seem to be calmly sitting still, but they're actually frozen in fear, and the longer they're terrified, the worse their chances.

You can check to see if Mom has visited the nest by draping a thread or two across the top of the nest. If it's moved by morning, she's been there. If she hasn't returned to the nest for 24 hours, then it's time to find your local wildlife rehabilitator and get expert help. The DEC, local veterinarians, or nature centers can locate a nearby rehabber, who generally specialize.

Similarly, baby birds who are bashing clumsily about in the yard, unable to fly, are probably just fine. There is a period of a week or so in which they are still learning how to fly, and strengthening their muscles with repeated attempts. Watch from a discreet distance and you'll likely see Mom check on her youngster, feeding and encouraging it. Some parents will even swoop down at cats or dogs in defense of their offspring.

Fortunately, Arthur is more inclined to chase snowballs than scout out rabbits. I spent another half hour throwing snowballs for him, some of which he even managed to retrieve intact. Then I coaxed Arthur to spit out the last snowball, and we went inside, where I faced the challenge of making a cup of hot tea with numb fingers. Meanwhile, Arthur shook snow all over the living room, drank a good big gulp of water, then came over to where I huddled on the sofa with my tea to share sloppy kisses. He's a good puppy.

Arthur Goes Kayaking on Dryden Lake

I like to blame my Golden Retriever when things don't go as I plan, and while he is likely to escalate any mishap into a total disaster (through no real fault of his own), the fact is, it's me who keeps putting us in crazy situations.

For instance, I decided I really, really wanted pictures of Arthur and me kayaking together, and Arthur agreed that this was a terrific idea.

Without allowing myself time to thoroughly evaluate the various ways this could end badly, I coaxed a friend into lending us her plastic kayak (I was smart enough not to use my own good one), and driving us to Dryden Lake. Ignoring Rhonda's common-sense advice to not attempt this insane stunt and her warning that I'd ride home in the back with the dog if we capsized, I handed her my camera, and with my friend's help we got the boat down to the slope of the launch site. Carefully keeping Arthur from walking into the gentle waves lapping at the shore, I got him into the kayak, slid in behind him, and accepted the paddle from Rhonda. She pushed us out into the water, and we were on our own.

"Arthur, sit, stay," I said in my most no-nonsense voice. He sat, and stayed, but looked around with excited interest. This doesn't sound like a big deal until you think about the effect his quick movements had on the stability of a kayak already sitting pretty low in the water.

I glanced at the brownish water, wrinkled my nose at the idea of going into it, and tried to paddle out far enough for pictures, while maintaining a deathgrip on Arthur's collar.

"Stay," I warned, as he looked over the side as if contemplating a swim. Arthur loves to swim. I don't mind swimming, but only if it's my idea and the water doesn't smell like dead snails. By some miracle I straightened the little kayak and looked toward Rhonda and the camera on shore, feigning a cheerful smile. Arthur's goofy grin was genuine.

Then Arthur spotted a fisherman on the opposite shore. The act of casting must have looked very much like the man was throwing something to my overachiever retriever, and I felt Arthur tense for a spring.

"Arthur! STAY!" I reproved, projecting authority over my anxiety, thinking it was a good thing Rhonda had insisted on bringing along several towels.

To my amazement and relief, Arthur calmed himself. More than anything, he wants to be a good puppy, and that was the only reason this harebrained idea had any chance of not ending in disaster.

Deciding that whatever photos Rhonda had managed to get in the three minutes we'd been out on the water would have to suffice, I let go of Arthur's collar to paddle as quickly as I could toward shore. The water moving alongside the boat caught Arthur's attention, and he leaned far over to investigate. The kayak tipped alarmingly, but somehow I got both Arthur and the boat back upright without letting any lake water inside.

One last stroke of the paddle put our prow up on the gravel of the boat launch, and my friend pulled us out. Only then did I allow myself a whoop of triumph. Coaxing Arthur away from the water's edge, I invited him to jump up on me -- the ultimate reward -- thumping his furry sides.

"We DID it! And we're both still dry!" I thought I couldn't be any prouder of my canine companion, until I had a chance to see the pictures. Despite the constant threat of imminent disaster combined with an unfamiliar camera, Rhonda had captured several priceless photographs. Of course, *she* hadn't been an inch away from smelling like a dirty frog bowl.

Arthur had no idea what he'd done to earn such praise, but with his typical joie de vivre, he revelled in the attention.

Arthur Thoroughly Enjoys Helping Recycle

When I purchased a new area rug, it came wrapped around a sturdy, eight-foot-long cardboard tube, like a paper towel core on steroids. I was going to cut it up and put it in with the rest of the recycling, but then decided it would be a terrific dog toy.

Inviting Arthur out on the lawn (where it's OK for an eighty-pound dog to get rambunctious), I showed this nifty novelty to him, and let him gently take it in his mouth, so he knew it was a toy he was allowed to play with. (It cuts down on misunderstandings, if you always make your dog wait for permission before letting him grab anything new.) After a few moments, I said, "Arthur, drop it," and he spit it out into my hands. Then I threw it javelin-style up the slight incline.

Off he raced, catching it in his teeth near one end, and circled back at a gallop, hampered by the way it dragged along the ground to one side. I threw it again, and this time he had wised up enough to catch it at the middle, balancing it nicely as he galumphed back toward me. But it was too light and awkward to throw very far, so it wasn't a very efficient way to exercise this energetic dog. After he retrieved it several times without doing it any more harm than a liberal soaking with dog spit, I decided that it was time to let him really play with it.

Hunters, obedience instructors, and practically every dog trainer with any experience will be horrified to know that I play tuggie with Arthur. They're perfectly correct: it's a terrible idea to allow your dog to fight you for possession of anything. Plus, it may encourage a dog to play tuggie with the retrieving dummy in a trial (or worse, that freshly-shot mallard out in the field) instead of releasing it gently to your hand.

The difference is, Arthur only gets to play tuggie on command. When I say *drop*, he instantly spits out whatever he's holding, even a dead quail, because he's learned that occasionally I have a treat for him. (The quickest way to teach a dog to let go of stuff is to give the command, then offer something better.)

But when I take hold of whatever Arthur has in his mouth and say, "Gimme that!" Arthur knows war has been declared, and all rules are out the window. He absolutely loves this game, and when I said the magic words and pulled on that cardboard tube, he threw his whole self, heart and soul and body, into trying to wrestle it away from me.

As a rug support, the tube served its purpose well; as a dog toy, it just didn't have what it takes to withstand the combination of Arthur's strong white teeth and that powerful body in the prime of life. The tube, weakened by its soaking in spit and never intended for this sort of mistreatment, parted in the middle with a satisfying ripping sound, which goaded Arthur into a frenzy of destruction.

Dropping the half he held in his jaws, he lunged for the piece I still had. Clamping his teeth down in a good solid grip, he braced his forefeet in the grass, chest low to the ground, rump high, tail wagging madly, and yanked sideways, first one way, then the other, growling happily as he ripped it apart.

(There's a big difference in dog growls. Arthur, like many dogs, will growl even while playing with toys all by himself. You can pet him, pull his fur and tug on his tail, and he's all just fun and play. The dog to beware of is the one who stands still, or walks stiff-legged toward you while staring you directly in the eye, growling low in his throat, even if his tail is wagging. A wagging tail does NOT mean a dog will not bite!)

Just to maintain some semblance of discipline, I suddenly stood up straight and let go of my end of the wet hunk of cardboard. "Arthur, drop."

He shook it a few times, then padded up to me, sat, and spit it out at my feet.

"EXcellent!" I told him, meaning it. "What a good puppy!" Then I picked up the longest relatively-intact piece of the badly-abused tube, and thwacked Arthur playfully in the ribs, saying "Gimme that!"

Instantly Arthur reverted back to destruct mode, closing his jaws on the tube and using both strength and body weight to twist the toy from my grasp. Again and again the tube gave up parts, until Arthur and I were sitting on the lawn, panting and happy, in the middle of a haphazard circle of torn shreds of wet cardboard.

If the worth of an object is decided by the sheer joy it brings, then this was a terrific dog toy with a free rug wrapped around it.

Arthur Takes a Doggy IQ Test

When my friend Kathy said she wished her beagle were as smart as my Golden, I pointed out to her that my dog would do several complicated tricks for a small piece of dry kibble, while Homer (yes, his name was Homer) could make her get off the sofa, go to the fridge, and offer him various food items until she happened upon one he liked.

Which dog do you consider smarter?

What is intelligence? We presume to measure it with some degree of precision in humans, but what about our canine family members?

Ah, the Internet is a wonderful resource (once you wade through all the junk), and it provided me with several tests to try on Arthur, all designed to be interesting and fun for both dogs and their humans.

The first requires only a treat and a paper towel. Make your dog sit-stay, then show him a small goodie, let him watch you set it in the middle of the floor, and cover it with the paper towel. Stand back and tell him, "Okay!"

Award your pup four points if he gets the treat within fifteen seconds, three if it takes half a minute, two for forty-five seconds, and one for over a minute. Zero points if he loses interest or eats the paper towel.

Arthur accidentally cheated on this one. He sniffed briefly at the edges of the paper towel, tail waving wildly, then he whirled around to look at me. His fluffy tail swept the paper towel aside, sending the treat skittering across the floor. He pounced on it and wolfed it down. I gave him the full four points because he did get it all by himself in less than five seconds.

All you need for the second test is a blanket. Pet your dog and talk to him enough to get him interacting but not wacko-idiot excited. When he's padding around, drape the blanket over him, covering his head and shoulders, and see what he does. He should be able to free himself easily. Use the same point system as above.

I was sure Arthur would fail this one, because I have a deplorable tendency to dress him up. But he surprised me by immediately dropping his head and shaking the blanket off. Arthur earned four points!

For the third test, you have to play dead. Yes, you, not the dog.

Pet your dog and get him wandering around happily. He has no idea that calamity will soon strike! All of a sudden, with no warning, you give a small cry, collapse on the floor and lay still. What does your dog do? Four points for trying to wake you. three if he goes for help, two if he barks, one for laying on you or standing protectively over you. Zero points if he runs to the cat dish and gobbles down Meow Mix.

Arthur immediately came over to peer down at me uncertainly, then dashed into the bedroom and returned with a disreputable stuffed toy. I have no idea how he thought Cookie Monster might help, but he meant well. I gave him a three.

The fourth test deals with memory: let your dog see you place a treat in a corner, then take him to another room and play with him for five minutes, the more exciting, the better. After five minutes, pat him and tell him he's a good puppy, dismissing him. He should go straight for the treat; award points like the first two tests.

The silent, ruthless presence of that biscuit completely distracted Arthur from the game of tuggie we were playing. Oh, he played, but without letting go of the toy we both held, he kept rolling his eyes toward the living room where the treat lay. It wasn't that he remembered it later; it's that he never quit thinking about it. Four points.

Tally up the score. Zero to five points is a special-needs pup; let him sleep on the bed. Six to eleven is average; he's up to the challenge of basic obedience training. Twelve to sixteen, be careful the *he* doesn't train *you*.

Surprisingly, Arthur scored higher than average ... and now that I think of it, he *has* trained me. When he comes over and shoves his snout under my hand, I almost always stop whatever I'm doing to pet him.

Most dogs love being the center of attention, and whatever the test might tell you about the workings of your chum's brain, he -- like Arthur -- will have a terrific time with these.

IQ is not a measure of worth. A dog who scores zero on every test could well be a more loving and devoted companion than one who aces the whole thing. I cherish Arthur regardless of his mental abilities (or occasional apparent lack thereof). And in return he loves me wholeheartedly, even when I push on a door clearly marked "Pull."

Arthur Adapts to Daylight Saving Time

Thanks to Daylight Saving Time, it's dark in the morning now when I take Arthur out for his constitutional. Ever since September twenty-third this year, the daylight hours have been getting shorter, while the hours of darkness have gotten longer -- good news for vampires, but not as handy for us diurnal daywalking folks, and my eighty-pound Golden Retriever pays the price in fun.

No more does Arthur get to run along ahead of me when we go outside, exploring the intriguing scents left by various critters during the night, as we head to the corner of the woods where he does his business. He has to hold himself in strict heel position while I sweep the surrounding area with a flashlight, because every once in awhile -- just often enough to keep me vigilant -- we see or smell a skunk in the backyard, and I suspect at least one raccoon has been helping himself to the dry cat food when I forget to pick it up at night.

And, as much as I love my beautiful dog, he isn't always the brightest bulb on the string. He firmly believes to the very core of his being that everyone he meets loves him, so he greets humans and animals alike as if they were long-lost friends in need of an enthusiastic welcome.

A raccoon would meet Arthur's friendly overtures with teeth and attitude, and while I doubt a skunk would resort to violence, I'm certain its nonviolent objection would be immediately effective, and I have no desire to see how well that concoction of baking soda, hydrogen peroxide and dish soap really works on a large and fluffy dog.

So, Arthur has to sit and stay, his curiosity twitching, while I peer into the gloom by the light of my small flashlight, making sure the coast is clear before he can jog out into the trees to do his thing every morning. Afterwards, when it was still light at that hour, he enjoyed galloping ahead as we went back to the house, but now he settles instead for pacing alongside me while I try to make it up to him by ruffling his ears and affectionately thumping his side. For Arthur, attention is better than any olfactory entertainment the yard has to offer.

After work, Arthur still needs exercise even though it's pitch dark out by six in the evening. The lone bulb over the front stoop only casts its weak oval of illumination as far as the driveway, leaving the big stretch of lawn where I usually throw Arthur's frisbee cast in murky twilight. But amazingly enough, being unable to see the frisbee doesn't stop him from catching it.

He simply trusts that it will be vaguely where he expects it, taking off before I throw the fabric toy, and his low-light vision must be much better than my own, because he neatly leaps up and catches it when I can't even clearly see *him*, much less a spit- and mud-stained piece of fabric barely a foot in diameter. Then he comes galumphing triumphantly back to stomp on my toes and deliver the sodden, smelly thing to my hand. Gee, thanks.

Even though he's willing to play fetch in the dark, Arthur still loses out because of the encroaching night. In the summer, when the sun on my face makes the breeze feel good, Arthur gets hot and exhausted rather quickly in that fur coat. Now that it's cooler, he's comfortable running around energetically, and would cheerfully keep at it for half an hour, while I'm standing there in the dark and the relentless wind, becoming hypothermic. Poor Arthur, some nights I don't even last ten minutes, and with winter looming, it's going to get worse before it gets better.

But here's a happy factoid about the seasons, which I discovered looking up the exact dates of the solstice and equinox: our planet doesn't maintain a constant speed throughout its journey around the sun, which means the four seasons are not quite equal. Here in the northern hemisphere, we enjoy spring and summer for 186 days, while fall and winter last less than 179. Believe it or not.

Still, the cold months *feel* longer, and I fully understand why people have celebrated the Winter Solstice for millennia. Arthur and I are both looking forward to December 21, and the gradual return of warmth and daylight.

Arthur Wags His Way Through Another Vet Visit

One evening about a week ago, I noticed that Arthur's toenails clicked on the hardwood floor as he padded cheerfully about. Time to trim them again, and while I was at it, the long tufts of fur on the ends of his toes that make him look like a character by Dr. Seuss, to help keep the floors clean.

No time like the present. I got out the scissors, a big emery board, and my doggy nail trimmers from Gramp. I've never seen pet nail clippers like these for sale. They're not the "guillotine" style widely available, but rather a side-to-side set of curved blades with the top enclosed. I have no idea how long Gramp had them, but they were well-worn when he gave them to me over fifteen years ago, and they still work great with only periodic light oiling. None of the newfangled inventions have ever improved on these simple, controllable trimmers.

You may think your dog isn't paying attention to every move you make, but he is. Even before I could call him, Arthur had noticed me, recognized the signs of an imminent belly rub, and was already wagging his way over.

"Arth, sit," I said softly, crouching by his side. He sat, and I sat on the floor behind him with one leg on either side of him, careful not to sit on his happily swishing tail. Then I pulled him over backwards onto me, so his head was in my lap and his feet in the air.

In addition to being a convenient position for a tummy rub and canine mani-pedi, this is also a test of your dog's temperament and his acceptance of your role as pack leader. At the first gentle pressure of my hands on his chest, Arthur passively allowed himself to be flipped upside-down, then lay there without moving, except for his tail sweeping an arc on the floor.

His trust and love warmed me through, even more than his eighty-pound furry self sprawled along the length of my body. I kissed his cold wet nose and whispered, *"EXcellent!"* and then of course, rubbed his pale golden tummy for a minute or two. Arthur squinted with joy, and panted in my face.

"Hmm, time to get your teeth cleaned, too," I commented, making a mental note to call the vet sometime soon. After doing his nails and clipping the fur between his toes, I slid out from under him, stepped out of the heap of nail-ends and fur, and in a very calm voice, told Arthur to come.

Ecstatic, he leaped up and lunged into heel position, scattering the debris far and wide. Well, the whole room had needed sweeping anyway. I petted him and assured him he was a good puppy, both verbally and edibly. I cleaned up, sat down, and went back to my tea and email, satisfied at having taken care of his nails for another few weeks.

When I heard Arthur come clicking back into the living room I realized it was more than just long nails. Carefully I watched him as he walked, and saw that he drags the tips of his back toes slightly, more on the left.

That wasn't good. All too aware that Arthur is no longer a young dog, I made a vet appointment and took the next day off work.

Arthur LOVES going to the vet. From his point of view, it's a building full of people who genuinely want to give him their undivided attention and lots of petting, which far outweighs the occasional needle or impolite procedure.

As long as they were going to put him under to x-ray his spine and legs, I asked them to remove the fatty tumor from the back of his neck and clean his teeth, two things I'd been meaning to have done anyway. It felt weird to leave him there, but he was enjoying a full body massage from one of the techs, and barely noticed my departure. He would be fine.

Only a little over six hours later, I picked him up. He seemed none the worse, except he had an incision with stitches across a shaved patch on his neck, and was much more sedate. (Turns out I was wrong, and don't want him calm. I want him to be himself, and I was vastly relieved the next day when he broke into his usual galumphing run on our way back inside the next morning.)

The toe-dragging is nothing to be alarmed about, especially since he can still run and jump to catch a frisbee eight feet in the air. Good riddance to the tumor, and I no longer have to turn my head when my chum pants in my face. I promised to be more diligent about brushing his teeth at home.

At Lucille's two days later, I told her what Arthur had done, plus a nugget I knew she would be glad to hear: "Oh, and the vet said Arthur could stand to gain a pound or two. I told him that was no problem, I'd just bring him up here to see you."

Lucille was glad to comply with the vet's advice, and so was Arthur.

While Humans Complain, Arthur Enjoys the Snow

I said a bad word when I peered out through the curtains this morning and saw a white car where I'd parked a dark green one last night. Ugh. Snow again already. I pulled on my boots and coat and mittens to take my golden retriever out for his morning constitutional.

Arthur usually waits politely for me to invite him to step through the open door. Today I only got as far as "Good pup--" before he exploded out of the house and onto the white lawn with delight. He snuffled and snorted, then demonstrated a classic Stop, Drop & Roll. Luckily the bitter overnight temperature had turned the mud into inert tundra, so when he stood and shook, his coat showed nearly no evidence at all that he had rolled; only the merry mess in the snow told the story of a happy dog having unbridled fun.

A little snow had turned the whole world into new territory, and Arthur padded cheerfully from shrub to tree to tuft of weeds, exploring all in their shroud of snow, sniffing and sneezing. A joyful dog is infectious, and Arthur was ecstatic. I couldn't help smiling at his delirious antics.

It was cold enough to justify warming the car, so as a special treat, I opened the back door of the car and told Arthur to hop in. Snow and a car ride! Arthur launched his 80 pound self, landing neatly on the blanket on the back seat. I started the motor and he flopped down, settling in for a ride.

Since I had to brush the snow off, I debated letting him stay in the car, but there have been too many horror stories in the news about pets and children suffocating when left inside running cars, even just while shoveling out a stuck tire. I opened the back door and lifted him out, then started using the snow brush to dust off my car.

I'm not sure what my efforts with the snowbrush looked like to Arthur, but his reaction was hilarious. Instead of trying to grab the wooden stick of the thing which might have been understandable, he jumped and bit at the snow as I cleared off the hood and back window. Dogs know how to thoroughly enjoy a good time without a care in the world for what anyone else thinks.

Finally the car was clean and Arthur was covered. As usual, he snuggled nice and close against my legs before shaking himself off. Now the car and Arthur were snow-free, and I suddenly had snow inside the collar of my coat, melting its way down the back of my neck. Arthur mistook my flailing arms and shriek of surprise as an invitation to jump up. Now I had snow down the front of my sweater too, but the discomfort was a small price to pay.

I scooped up a handful of fluffy snow, and held it in my bare hand long enough to warm it into a snowball (and numb my fingers), then threw it across the front lawn, where it disappeared. Instantly Arthur was after it, wagging madly as he searched it out by thrusting his whole face into the snow, shaking his head and starting again a few feet away. In summertime, his search efforts may seem random, but with snow on the ground, I could see he was actually quartering the area effectively, if not methodically.

To no one's surprise, he found the snowball and turned to gallop toward me like a freight train, as I crouched and welcomed him with my arms wide in the ultimate wordless signal for "come." Also as expected, he ran me over and I lay there on my back on the hard frozen ground, with him standing over me triumphantly, protectively, expectantly.

"Excellent," I murmured into the wet furry face pressed against my own. "You. Are. Excellent." My coat was covered in snow now, and smelled slightly of wet dog, but I didn't care.

There are many ways dogs enhance our lives: first and foremost, their honest love for us despite our faults; the way they extract so much enjoyment from simple things like snow; the mere act of petting them lowers our blood pressure; making sure they get enough exercise helps us get some, too; caring for them makes us feel needed; even a small dog increases our sense of safety (my dog doesn't have to defend me, he just has to alert me so I can defend us both); and the quiet sense of companionship and belonging, when your dog is sleeping on the sofa with his head in your lap.

To someone who has never had a dog (or cat, or what have you), it may not seem like a sleeping fuzzy critter drooling on your pajamas can substantially improve your life, but I assure you, I can't imagine living without one.

Arthur Outlasts his Human During a Tracking Exercise

It suddenly hit me that on Valentine's Day, Arthur will be seven years old, and I felt a fresh wave of guilt for not giving him the opportunity to reach more of his potential.

Sometimes I feel like a waste of this amazing dog. Not only is he sweet, loving, and beautiful due to his many red-letter show-champion ancestors, but among the lengthy list of letters following his sire's name is the simple term "TC" —Tracking Champion.

Arthur has inherited his famous father's tracking talent, but I've only ever really played with it, as if it were a parlor trick on par with getting a soda from the fridge, doing square roots, and opening the car door. But tracking is much more than that. One well-trained dog with this gift can mean the difference between life and death for a person lost in the woods.

For years I've meant to contact a local tracking club, but never quite got around to it. Seeing Arthur approach the halfway point in an average dog's life, I couldn't put it off any longer.

This past week I contacted the Northeast branch of a nationwide association of independent search and rescue canine handlers, and made a doggie date for Arthur to show his stuff to a certified rescue team next Sunday. Only then did it occur to me that Arthur hasn't actually tracked a person in months.

So on Sunday I decided it would be great fun to take Arthur out tracking, and my friend Rhonda volunteered to lay the trail. Although I consider myself fairly intelligent, some of my decisions have sure been doozies.

Oh, there was never any chance Arthur would be unable to find Rhonda, especially under such perfect conditions: we had an article of clothing, knew exactly where to start, and nobody had confused the trail by walking back and forth over the scent. The foot of snow on the ground was a plus, covering a lot of potentially distracting scents.

At least I thought the heavy, wet snow was a plus, before I actually attempted to jog through the stuff behind my excited dog. That was my first mistake.

My second mistake was drastically underestimating Rhonda's physical condition, and my third was overestimating my own out-of-shape abilities. I've never been able to keep up with Arthur while tracking, but I've always been able to run-stumble more or less with him with the leash wrapped around my hand. Today I felt like a ragdoll tied to a runaway locomotive, and had to make him stop and wait for me to gasp air back into my burning lungs several times.

During one of my rests, as I stood hunched over with one hand on my knees and one on Arthur's fuzzy head, I noticed that the snow which had caked onto my jeans in the first few dozen yards had melted, soaking into the denim, and had now re-frozen, turning my lower legs into jeansicles. Terrific. I straightened and continued on.

Across a stubbly cornfield we went, me huffing and puffing, Arthur yearning joyfully at the end of the leash.

Finally the woods loomed ahead. Rhonda *couldn't* have gone much farther, could she?

Apparently, yes she could. Up what seemed to be a sheer cliff we went, Arthur doing most of the work getting me to the top. But we still saw no sign of Rhonda! How far could she have hiked in this amorphous, sentient and malevolent snow? Arthur and I must have gone at least five miles already! (In fact, I later determined that our entire round trip was probably close to a mile and a half.)

Arthur dragged me on a circuitous path through the woods until finally, *finally* we found Rhonda hiding behind a shrub. Relieved, I unwound the leash from my numb hand and sank exhausted onto a snow-covered branch, dizzy and out of breath but immensely proud of my beloved chum. "Good pup, Arth," I wheezed asthmatically. "Excellent." My happiness only lasted until I realized we still had to hike back to the car, and that now my butt was cold, too.

Once I caught my breath again, I felt a little better, and since we were already out in a field, I wanted to try something I've never been able to do with Arthur: see if he could track *me*, with someone else holding the leash. Luckily, Rhonda is not only in great shape, she's patient, and cheerfully agreed to yet another hike in the snow and cold.

Promising to keep it short (although I was the only one tired), I handed Rhonda one of my mittens as a scent item, putting my bare hand in my coat pocket. Then, leaving Rhonda and Arthur in a shallow little valley in the cornfield, I trudged up the hill and down the other side, then ducked into the woods along a deer path.

This time I was not testing Arthur's abilities; I knew he could find me. But would he obey and behave for Rhonda? I huddled in a crouch among the barren trees, wheezing as quietly as possible, and waited.

—and waited. What was taking so long?

Then all of a sudden there they were, Arthur bounding with limitless energy through snow as high as his shoulders, Rhonda doing a much better job of not hindering him than I had. Arthur greeted me with justifiable satisfaction and delight, and I petted and made much of him, pretending to be much more alive than I felt.

The trek back out was easier, with Arthur walking sedately at heel.

At home I took the ice balls off Arthur's feet and legs and tummy; then there was nothing I wanted to do more than take a hot shower and curl up under a blanket, and Arthur agreed that a Sunday afternoon nap was a great decision.

Arthur Searches for the Ernie in a Hayfield

In an effort to keep our training sessions interesting for both my golden retriever and myself (and because we're running out of new participants willing to help with tracking), Sunday morning I decided to take Arthur's Ernie toy out for a walk in the field near the house, and leave it there until evening (having previously obtained the kind permission of the landowners.)

If the neighbors noticed and wondered why I was wandering in aimless broad loops in knee-deep snow, carrying a scruffy preschool toy, they didn't come out and ask. I suppose I wouldn't have, either. Deliberately I crossed and re-crossed my own path to make the trail more challenging, until out in the middle of this five-acre snowscape, I dropped Ernie into one of my footprints, scuffed some snow on top of it, and continued on, finally making my way back to the house. I took my boots off, dumped the snow out of them, brushed off what hadn't melted into my jeans, and went inside to the welcome warmth to thaw.

Hours later, I called Arthur out to the kitchen and showed him his bell. Unlike tracking a person, where I stumble along holding his leash, when I send him out to find a missing item, I affix a bell to his collar with a twist tie and let him have at it on his own. The bell keeps me apprised of his general whereabouts, and a silent dog whistle provides instant recall if necessary.

At sight of the familiar bell, Arthur went wild. He loves this game, and trembled with the herculean effort required to hold himself still long enough for me to put the bell on his collar. This only takes about five seconds, but that's at least an hour in dog years, so as soon as I was done, I told him he was a good puppy and let him outside to run some of the idiocy off before taking him out back to the hayfield, where Ernie waited patiently.

After Arthur had dashed around, eaten some snow, rolled in a drift, and marked his territory, I called him to heel and took him to where my earlier tracks started. Pointing, I set him off with the words: "Arthur, find it!"

Instantly he exploded into a frenzy of activity, questing back and forth, nose to snow, tail wagging so hard I thought it must hurt his ribs when it lashed against his sides. Suddenly, he found my trail and started out at a purposeful trot, the whole lower half of his face thrust into the snow, sneezing and shaking his head occasionally as he went, the bell making a happy sound.

Quickly I pulled my camera from my pocket, set it to video mode and turned it on. I love showing off how clever he --

"Arthur, no!" I yelled, turning off the video. As if aware I was recording his performance for posterity, Arthur had quit following my footprints and playfully thrown himself onto his back, making doggy snow angels -- smack in the middle of a burdock patch. Reluctantly, regretfully, he desisted and stood.

"Arthur," I said, pointing vaguely toward the open field. "Find the Ernie."

I'm not sure if he identifies this particular toy by name, like his tennis ball and teddy bear, but he certainly knows the word "find." Back out he went, picking up almost exactly where he'd left the trail, all business now, and I turned the camera back on. Nosing his way across the field, he found the spot where I'd hidden the toy, dived in up to his shaggy shoulders, and came up with something colorful and fuzzy clutched triumphantly in his jaws.

"EXCELLENT!" I called, laughing. Without even taking the time to shake the snow off his face, Arthur bounded through the snow in a straight line toward me, delirious with joy. I turned off the camera before he could nose-print the lens (again) and pocketed it as we went back to the house, Arthur dancing around me as we walked.

I wiped him off with the towel on the porch, picked ice balls from between his toes and pronounced him fit to enter the house. Since I hadn't trudged through the deep snow myself this time out, my feet were still warm and dry, and only my fingers were slightly chilled. Even Ernie was none the worse for wear, other than needing to spend the night drying in front of the heater.

Later, after I'd taken a hot shower and was ready for bed, I frowned to see Arthur chewing at the thick fur of his tail, and only then remembered the burdocks. Rats. I pulled a long coat on over my flannel pajamas, and by flashlight pulled the embedded burs off my dog in the driveway.

Trimming Nails

It was about 2 AM when I heard it again: tick, tick, tick. Tick, tick, tick. Back and forth, as my Golden Retriever paced. Arthur needed his nails trimmed. Again.

Wooden floors have many advantages, including natural beauty; dog fur sweeps up easily; and fleas have nowhere to hide or lay eggs. But there is one glaring drawback to this convenient flooring: unless I'm scrupulous about cutting Arthur's nails, when he can't sleep, neither can I.

I use a pair of dual-edge doggy nail trimmers and one of those big "professional" emery boards you can find at any dollar store. The emery board is the most important; you can, with patience, file down a skittish dog's nails without recourse to clippers at all.

That sharp *click!* sound causes some dogs extreme distress, perhaps in the same way we feel uneasy hearing fingernails dragging down a chalkboard. It doesn't physically hurt, but it's certainly not comfortable. Dogs can be particularly nervous about nail-trimming if they've ever had the quick nicked (the vein inside a dog's toenail is called the "quick.")

Even if your dog is as complaisant as Arthur the Marshmallow, an emery board is indispensible. Instead of just one or two big clips, taking many little nibbles at the nail will help lower your chances of cutting into the quick, and minimize sharp edges, but any size dog with freshly-trimmed nails putting all his weight and energy directly on top of your bare instep isn't any fun. Eighty-pound Arthur has wrung inadvertent yelps of pain from me (if anyone knows where to buy steel-toed bunny slippers, please contact me.) Small lapdogs can inflict even worse damage, because we tend to hold them in our arms. So filing their nails after clipping is a must.

What about that nifty electric puppy pedicure thingy they advertise on TV? Well, the commercial cleverly cuts the sound out while they're demonstrating their product in action. Why? Because it's basically a Dremel tool with a clear plastic guard. Unless your dog has complete faith and trust in you, as well as nerves of steel, any attempt to hone his nails down with this contraption is going to lead to some ugly displays of fear and temper, which could set a bad example for the dog.

The easiest method I've found so far is to sit on the floor behind the dog, and pull him over backwards into my lap. For most dogs, this is the happy tummy-rub position -- and at the subconscious level, it's a very submissive posture, triggering his instinct to submit and let the alpha (me) do whatever I want. All four feet are easily accessible, toenail-side-up, and the dog can't lean his full weight on me. He can pull his foot back, but I let him go ahead and draw his foot in as far as it can go against his body, and I can still work on the nails with no problem.

Of course, the ideal time to attempt anything new and potentially stressful is before dinner but after you've exercised your dog to exhaustion, not at two AM when you're sleep-dazed and groggy, with a flashlight between your teeth, and he's been wide-awake and antsy for an hour (or however long it took for the click-click-clicking to wrench you from bed before you went mad, utterly mad.) This way your canine chum comes to the project with his maximum attention span, and afterwards you can use dinner as a reward -- the tried-and-true recipe for a positive training experience.

Also, it's worth noting that you should also try to only clip your dog's nails while you're wearing scruffy jeans and a t-shirt, and don't mind getting a little dirty. It seems a bit pointless to take a nice long, hot shower with rose-scented soap, spray on a little cologne and slip into your best set of silky pajamas, only to crawl out of your nice warm bed a little while later to go sit on the floor with a lapful of dog who hasn't had a bath in weeks.

Arthur Learns the Difference Between
Gray Squirrels and Reds

The two gray squirrels that were here when we moved in have now multiplied into at least seven, plus at least two red squirrels, all in varying stages of denial that my ten-year-old Golden Retriever is, in fact, a dog.

If the gray squirrels run, he will sometimes give chase, just for form's sake, but it's halfhearted at best, and he halts as he's supposed to at the road (such as it is.) Some of the squirrels have noticed this and now stop just across the street, about ten feet away from him, lashing their bushy tails at him. The more savvy and brazen ones refuse to run at all; they sit right there radiating silent disapproval, and he halts in disconcerted surprise as they deliberately continue eating while maintaining eye contact, just to prove their point.

The gray squirrels are big and sociable, squabbling amiably amongst themselves until they settle on who gets to sit on top of the inverted birdbath (situated as we are between a lake and a canal, the birds are not attracted to a bath, so I turned it upside-down for a nice flat feeding station), who eats from the squirrel feeder, and who has to swing wildly back and forth from the hanging birdfeeder to get a snack. I've photographed seven eating peacefully within a few feet of each other.

Red squirrels, also delightfully known as *chickarees* after one of the many sounds they make, are the Mafia of the squirrel world. A third the size of the grays, just one red can and will chase several bigger gray squirrels off the feeders, swearing horribly at them in Squirrelese. This loud growly sound needs no translation, and my gentle Arthur doesn't even pretend to chase these guys.

They are highly territorial toward other red squirrels, and I usually only see one at a time, except when one is chasing another with surprising ferocity. Female red squirrels come into heat only for one day in late winter and again in early summer, and those are the only times she will allow another red squirrel in her territory, although females occasionally give up part of their area to their offspring.

In thirty-five days she bears three to seven hairless, blind young, which are weaned at six to eight weeks. Only about one-fifth of these babies will live to see their first birthday, when they're old enough to raise their own family.

Both gray and red squirrels are in the same family as chipmunks and woodchucks, but it's the red squirrels who have zero respect for personal property. They're the ones who've chewed away whole hunks of my bird-proof squirrel feeder. Not that the grays haven't nibbled the edges of the plastic birdfeeder, but red squirrels totally demolished a wooden feeder I was foolish enough to spread peanut butter on.

That aggressive self-confidence, however, makes the red squirrels endearingly approachable. I've gotten close enough to pet them when they're young and stupid – a really, *really* bad idea, by the way, as their long yellow teeth bear a striking resemblance to wirecutters. One enterprising chap decided to sleep right inside the feeder one rainy, thundery night, assuring himself of a dry and secure spot to wait out the storm, with the prospect of breakfast in bed.

Arthur isn't really much practical help while I clean and fill the feeders every evening, but his happy golden presence makes everything brighter, and while I might be done faster if he wasn't helping, it wouldn't be nearly as much fun.

Yes, Arthur, There's a Doggy Santa, Too

Christmas can be a stressful time for housepets as well as people: shattered routines, erratic behavior on the part of their usually comfortably predictable humans, strangers coming and going, odd items in unusual places, familiar items altered or removed altogether.

Your dog (or cat, or whatever critter shares your life) will be happier if you make a deliberate effort to maintain at least one or two accustomed activities, such as their morning walk or ear-scritching, plus a few minutes set aside for some one-on-one attention in the evening. You'll find that a bit of quiet time with your animal companion can benefit you, too, significantly reducing your chances to take a hammer to the radio when you hear that $56,712^{th}$ rendition of "Jingle Bell Rock."

With a little care, the holiday season can also be fun for pets. Generally, humans celebrate with food, and Christmas is one of the best opportunities for a housepet to cadge treats from people primed to be generous by the munificent mood of the season.

Unfortunately, not everything that's tasty is healthy. A few tiny treats -- and I mean *tiny*; Arthur gets morsels the size of my thumbnail -- won't hurt if his usual diet is a high-quality commercial food.

However, it's important to be aware that at this time of year, veterinarians see a disproportionate number of animals suffering from "dietary indescretion." In other words, it's not just a matter of the potential weight gain, although obesity is as much a health risk for pets as it is for humans. The trouble is, what's safe for you isn't necessarily safe for them.

For instance, "chocolate to die for" isn't an exaggeration for dogs. They love the stuff, but it can kill them. Symptoms include throwing up, overheating, seizures, and death. Wrapping chocolate up before putting it under the tree only makes it a fun challenge. Remember, law enforcement officers use dogs every day to sniff out well-hidden drugs that the dogs have zero desire to eat; your chum can certainly smell a food item he craves through a couple layers of cardboard and paper. A dog can and will rip open a gift-wrapped box and eat an entire pound of Gertrude Hawk Black Forest Truffles, and possibly the ribbon and paper as well.

Pancreatitis is another grave concern, often brought on by eating too much fat. The pancreas goes into overdrive and actually begins digesting itself and the organs around it. While your dog would cheerfully polish off the fatty trimmings from the roast, a few seconds of pleasure are not worth paying for with a painful death. Don't forget to make sure the garbage can is secure.

Keep all food safely out of reach, gifts or otherwise. (The countertop, by the way, is well within the reach of many dogs and most cats.) A new artificial sweetener called xylitol, found in frostings, gum, and other products, has caused canine deaths. Grapes seem innocent, but can be deadly. Eating a one-pound box of raisins can kill an eighty-pound retriever.

Another hazard of the holidays is choking. Many dogs, Arthur emphatically included, wolf down treats with such enthusiasm that they don't take the time to chew. I always cringe to see Arthur hack and gasp when he swallows an entire biscuit without crunching it first. He's no longer allowed chewies at all, rawhide or otherwise, because he only mouths them briefly, getting them wet and slimy enough to gag down whole. When I spotted a green toothbrush-shaped chewie almost completely intact in one of his deposits on the lawn, that was the last he ever got.

Food isn't the only thing animals can choke on. Christmas decorations offer a multitude of small items your cat or dog may find tempting to taste, if only because they're a novelty. Poinsettias, while generally not lethal, may make your furry companion vomit, and nobody wants to spend Christmas morning cleaning up that.

Cats are notorious for eating tinsel off the tree, a seasonal variant on the rubber band snacks enjoyed by many felines, including Merlin, my Aunt Gerry's sweet and beautiful ragdoll. Electrical cords, such as those for the lights on the tree, are especially dangerous if the animal can crouch beneath the tree and gnaw unnoticed until both wires connect with his conductive self.

Then there's the presents. Arthur loves to shred the paper from them with glee, scattering improvised confetti throughout the living room. If you indulge your dog in this fashion by wrapping his gifts, just make sure he doesn't eat any of the wrapping paper or ribbon, or move on to someone else's present. Ever helpful, Arthur would love to unwrap everyone's gifts, and I suspect he enjoys the process of opening his toys more than playing with them.

Lastly but most importantly, never give a pet of any kind as a surprise present, unless you are personally prepared to take on the responsibility of that animal's care for the entire length of his or her lifetime.

It takes only a few minutes and a little foresight to make sure Christmas is safe as well as merry for our furry friends. Everyone will be happier, and the vet may get to enjoy the holiday home with their family.

Many thanks to Dr. Martin and staff for contributing valuable advice and ideas to this column.

Arthur Enjoys Special Attention as an Older Dog

My nine-year-old Golden Retriever rested his chin on the edge of the bed, and peered imploringly up at me with those dark, soulful eyes.

"OK, Arth," I invited him up. With more gritty determination than grace he scrambled up, and elbow-scootched his way across the bed to lay his head on my foot and nudge hard. This is his idea of a subtle hint to pet him.

Obligingly I stroked his silky fur, noting with the usual helpless fear the white mask spreading across his face. Big dogs don't tend to live as long as smaller ones, and even though Arthur comes from a carefully-bred line that includes longevity as well as beauty, intelligence, and gentleness, still, Arthur is no longer in his prime, and like any older soul, dog or human, he requires some extra care to prevent problems.

One of the first symptoms of old age is joint problems and reduced mobility. The same glucosamine and chondroitin combination that humans take for joint health is available for dogs, and fortunately either it tastes good, or (more likely) Arthur has an alarmingly broad definition of "edible." He loves the tablets we got from the vet, and there are no bad side effects when this supplement is taken at the dose your veterinarian recommends. (There is also a rather fishy-smelling version for cats.)

Another way to help your chum get the most enjoyment out of his older years is to help him get out of a car or down off the furniture. If he leaps headfirst down onto a slippery floor, especially when excited, it's all too easy for one of his legs to slide, causing damage to ligaments and joints. Fortunately this is totally preventable.

One of my basic rules is to only have animals I can physically lift; an 80 lb dog is pushing the limits of my abilities, but I can pick Arthur off the bed and set him gently on the floor. Teaching your dog to wait for you to lift him down has the added advantage of keeping everything at a low excitement level, and solidifies his trust in you. It does, however, increase the amount of dog hair on your clothes, but if you're worried about that, you probably don't let your dog on the furniture to start with.

Even more important is assisting him when he gets out of a car. Obviously, if he's in a truck or SUV, it's only common sense to lift him to the ground. If he's in the back seat of a Honda Civic, there isn't as much risk to his joints (unless there's ice) but there is a *huge* safety factor in teaching your dog to wait for you to physically lift him out: he doesn't launch himself out of the car the moment you open the door. Everybody benefits from your dog waiting for permission and/or help getting out of the car, especially the dog.

Another thing which you should have been doing all along is keeping him at a healthy weight, and exercising him regularly. If your dog is fat, you're probably not getting enough exercise either, so take him out in the yard and toss a toy, or throw a frisbee. If your dog is one of those who readily chases and retrieves things, but then refuses to relinquish them, try giving the command "Drop" and then offering a small piece of bacon. Chances are your pup will spit out the toy with alacrity.

Pay attention to his habits, and if anything seems out of the ordinary, consult a vet. I have never said, "gee, I wish I hadn't taken that animal to the vet." In fact, I have a friend who noticed that her dog was turning around in more circles than normal before laying down. Sound silly? It worried her enough that she took him in for x-rays, and they found a tumor! Luckily it was in an early stage, and the surgery was a success. Ben enjoyed several years that he might not have had, if she had waited for more tangible symptoms.

Enjoy your dog's golden years, and go ahead, let him up on the furniture. If fussy friends comment on the dog hair, it's time to find new friends.

Arthur and the Snow Geese

Last Wednesday I took the day off work for several reasons: a USDA inspection for my educational animals license, my car desperately needed the muffler or something fixed -- and, most importantly, Arthur had just had minor surgery on Tuesday to remove a small lump on his gum above his upper right fang.

My beautiful companion turned ten on Valentine's Day (yes, we had a party.) Like many dogs, as he's gotten older, he has had several lumps and an odd wart or two. The one on his neck had turned out to be just a fatty tumor, and the vet assured me that this one was probably just overactive gum tissue, but ought to be removed and sent for biopsy.

Happily, Arthur was sent home with absolutely no restrictions, and since they had cauterized the area, he didn't even need antibiotics. I breathed a sigh of relief, and looked out Wednesday morning at a blue sky and sun. I dropped off the car, gave the house a once-over, and then we had hours ahead of us, and absolutely nothing to do but explore a nearby seasonal road.

There are people who claim to like Spring; I am not one of them. Spring means mud, ice, and damp cold wind. Arthur schlooped through the morass that used to be my driveway, instantly turning from a pale gold thoroughbred to a wet brown mutt from the belly down. The walk to the seasonal road was no less messy. I patted my companion's head and reassured myself that he'd clean up in the snow.

Dale had conveniently driven his big tractor down the road fairly recently, his wide tires leaving a nice double path for me. Arthur, of course, needed no path, and frankly preferred the clean unbroken snow to the sides of the road for his doggy snow angels.

He made lots of them, inadvertently scrubbing himself clean as he twisted and rolled with glee in the snow while I watched with pleasure as he gradually turned gold again.

"Excellent!" I said, crouching down with my arms wide. This is the ultimate recall "command" -- an invitation to be hugged. Arthur scrambled to his feet, not even taking time to shake off before galloping toward me like a freight train.

Stepping a little to one side at the moment before collision, I laughed and hugged his wildly wagging self, making a mental note that although he looked clean, he would definitely benefit from a bath with scented shampoo. Calming down after a few minutes, Arthur shook himself vigorously, then took off down the tractor path, delighted with life. Wondering if my coat really means it when it says, "Dry clean only," I hiked along after him, taking pictures.

At the top of a little hill, I heard geese overhead and looked up as a ragged V of Canada Geese noisily made their way toward the lake. What a racket! Then I saw the Snow Geese.

A flock of migrating geese is called a "skein" for its resemblance to a piece yarn. These were white birds in the bright sunlight against an azure sky, and the rhythmic flapping of their wings made them sparkle and shimmer. It was beautiful.

Arthur showed zero interest in the geese, not even the ones landing in the cornfield only a few yards away. He snuffled in the snow, unconcerned at the growing din, but I decided it was time to go.

My fuzzy puppy stayed clean until we got to the real road. In an effort to prevent him from galumphing down the middle of the sloppy mess, I called him to heel, and we minced our way along the edge. That worked until we got to my driveway. With a sigh of resignation, I said, "Okay."

Gleefully Arthur padded back and forth in the mud. Ah, well, he needed a bath anyway. No time like the present.

"Come on, pup," I called, and we went inside.

Our new luxury is a shower stall with a hand-held spray nozzle. Without really thinking it through, I introduced Arthur to the shower with small cubes of cheese and plenty of affection and encouragement. He was fine with it, and stood quietly, his sodden tail waving gently as I wet him down, soaped him up, and rinsed him off.

The show-dog command "Stand, stay" has practical applications outside a show ring. Arthur stood stock-still as I vigorously towelled him off, got a new towel, and towelled some more. If you aren't tired and out of breath after drying a big furry dog with a towel, you didn't do a thorough job.

That evening during my own shower, I realized that giving Arthur praise and petting and treats during his bath might not have been such a brilliant idea. As I basked in the hot spray with my eyes closed, suddenly Arthur was right there beside me in what was now a very tiny space. His whole body wagged with anticipation of approval.

"Good puppy," I said, because he had only done exactly what I had praised him for earlier. This was my fault, for not making it clear that showers are strictly one-at-a-time. From now on I'll have to close the bathroom door.

Arthur Helps Build a Modern Stone Circle

A stone circle, by definition, is pretty much any arrangement of stones in a circle. (A true "henge" has a bank outside the stones, and a ditch within.) I've always wanted a small version of a stone circle in my own backyard, so I decided to build one.

A local farmer didn't mind in the slightest if I took eight good-size rocks from the edge of his field (although he did give me a rather odd look when I explained what they were for), so I invited my Golden Retriever to go for a drive to help me choose rocks.

Arthur watched with utter incomprehension as I sorted through the small mountain of debris, where the farmers have been dumping rocks from the fields for generations. He had zero interest in rocks, and did not understand why I hadn't brought his Flippy Flopper toy, a customary accessory on our walks. He soon started snuffling around in the weeds by the shallow wetland nearby, enjoying a kaleidoscope of scents invisible to us mere humans.

There were so many stones of acceptable size that I had a difficult time narrowing it down to just eight, but eventually I settled on several with interesting striations, some with odd shapes, one with sparkly mica (?) throughout, and I was especially pleased to find one full of fossils.

Transferring my choices into the car, I looked around for Arthur. He never goes far, and I had heard chuffing and a sneeze or two, which meant he must be having a good time.

He sure was. My ten-year-old puppy was making mud angels at the edge of the swamp.

"Arth--" I began, then winced, and let him do whatever he wanted, as I have been for the past month. He could get as dirty as he liked, do anything that made him happy.

"Good puppy," I said, and took pictures.

The biopsy on the small growth removed from his gum had come back with the ominous phrase "amelanotic melanoma" – an unusual form of malignant cancer. The specialist vet up in Baldwinsville didn't have anything good to say, except that we had caught it early enough that he wanted to try a second surgery.

This time he had to remove Arthur's upper right fang and several other teeth, as well as part of his jaw. Several days later, biopsies from the edges came back clean, which meant he had gotten it all. So far, so good.

Unfortunately, mouth tissue is very delicate, and although I've temporarily picked up all his stuffed toys and put away the fabric frisbee, Arthur is still an ebullient, enthusiastic guy. The stitches pulled out. Back he went for new stitches, which also pulled out. At that point, the vet decided that instead of putting Arthur through anesthesia for a fourth time in three weeks, it was better to just let it heal on its own.

He sent us home with an orange-flavored mouth rinse, a biweekly checkup schedule, instructions to watch for any sign of infection (Arthur had already done a ten-day course of antibiotics and painkillers), and the vet's own personal cell phone number.

So, I've been letting Arthur get away with everything from peeing on the rose bushes to sleeping in my spot on our bed. If he hogs the pillow, I just use him instead. While I'm pretty sure Arthur has noticed this sudden, drastic relaxation of rules, he's too well-mannered to take full advantage of it, although half a sandwich disappeared mysteriously from the tea-table the other day.

Throughout this entire experience, Arthur himself has continued to act reassuringly cheerful and affectionate (especially after a big sloppy drink of water) with his usual seemingly endless energy.

After we got back home, I envied him his energy as I watched him bounce around in the litter of last year's leaves. Wondering if I should maybe try whipping up a batch Cream of Iams soup for myself, I transferred my eight very heavy prizes from the car to the little clearing in the woods behind the house.

Arthur supervised as I arranged them on the compass points using a twenty-foot string to maintain a nice circle, using a stump as the center. The fossil rock I gave pride of place directly in line with the setting sun, so anyone curious enough can figure out the exact date I did this.

The special interest I showed this one stone, carefully cleaning the dirt from its nifty ancient shell shapes, drew Arthur's attention to it. Before I could guess his intent, he christened my stone circle – and all I could do was laugh.

Arthur Gets His Toys Back

Two Saturdays ago, my golden retriever had his final follow-up with the specialist vet up in Baldwinsville, after the surgeries to remove a cancerous tumor in his jaw. Weekends at any veterinary clinic often consist of back-to-back crises, so seeing Arthur, a happy and now healthy dog, was a genuine bright spot for the vet. As a parrot shrieked in the background, sounding like it was dying by inches (in fact it was merely getting its nails and beak trimmed; I asked) Dr. Spindel peered in Arthur's mouth with a flashlight and justifiable self-satisfaction, and declared him completely healed.

"So he can have his toys back? And play Frisbee again?" I wanted to make sure.

"Yep," the vet agreed, grinning and petting the insistent retriever, who was vigorously shedding on his dark slacks. Arthur is one of his favorite patients, this big bearlike retriever who loves going to the vet. To Arthur, this is an entire building full of people who pet him and tell him he's a good puppy, even if he breaks *stay* and steps on their feet.

It had been heartbreaking to pick up all of Arthur's plush toys after his mouth surgery, but necessary. Nor could he be allowed to grab even his relatively soft fabric frisbee with his gums stitched and healing. Depriving a retriever of things to retrieve is a terrible thing to do. I tried to make up the loss by taking him for longer walks, and giving him more one-on-one time, but I knew he missed his toys.

So Saturday as soon as we got home, I brought all of his freshly-laundered stuffed toys out of the cupboard, and dumped them in a heap in front of him. It had been over two months since he'd seen a toy.

I'll never forget his reaction. For just a moment, he stood there dumbfounded, staring in amazement and a total inability to decide which first. Then he pounced into the pile, tail waving deliriously, coming up with a colorful caterpillar from Lucille, which has always been one of his favorites (even though it long ago lost its glued-on felt spots to the washing machine.)

Snorting with joy, Arthur wagged over to me with the silly thing, his eyes bright and ears up, tail hitting his sides in his excitement. "But wait, there's more," I quipped, pulling two Flippy Floppers from the cupboard as well.

Right before I discovered the tumor, I had ordered a new fabric frisbee to replace the much-abused old one. When the new one arrived days after his surgery, I put it away with a pang in my heart, not sure if he'd ever be able to play with it. I also left his old one in the washing machine through several loads of laundry, and it had rehabilitated surprisingly well. Arthur doesn't actually chew on his toys, he just soaks them with dog drool then drops them in dirt, rather like dipping zucchini in egg and then breadcrumbs, but with less appealing results.

Now he had not just one, but two frisbees! I took him out to the back yard and threw the old one first. He couldn't believe his eyes at sight of the flying fabric disc, his favorite item in all the world. Dropping the caterpillar (which I hadn't had the heart to make him leave inside), he galumphed across the yard and leaped up, missing spectacularly. He picked it up and started toward me, and I let him get about halfway back before I threw the second one. It's fun to overload his brain with happiness.

I'd like to say he caught the second Flippy Flopper, but nope, he missed that one as well, although he tried with all his heart and soul. Clearly, we needed to practice. With a chuckle, I hoofed out to retrieve the first one as he danced around in ecstasy.

We invested another twenty minutes or so relearning how to catch a frisbee in midair, only quitting when he finally caught three in a row. By then we were both tired and happy and ready for some ice cream.

Because oh, yes, the vet also said Arthur could eat anything he wants. (I promise, we'll resume a reasonably healthful diet after some much-deserved celebratory supertreats.)

Arthur spent the evening carrying all the different toys around, dropping the one in his mouth for the next one he saw. Once again, I'm tripping over a dozen or so toys in varying stages of disrepute strewn randomly about the house. I'd missed them, too.

Arthur and the Fuzzy Football

My ten-year-old Golden Retriever cheerfully trotted across the kitchen toward me with his fuzzy football engulfed in his mouth. This scruffy toy he had decided to inherit by the simple expedient of pilfering it from the bookshelf where I had sentimentally kept it after my first Golden, Arthur's uncle, had passed away. It had been one of Hobby's favorite toys, and looked it: misshapen and worn, with its tag in tatters.

But when I accepted it from him, I noticed a slight swelling on top of his snout.

Trying very hard not to panic, I called the vet and made an appointment for the next day. Arthur had already undergone three surgeries for an aggressive sort of cancer.

On the way to the vet's, Arthur leaped lightly to the front seat as was his wont, and I absently circled his neck with my right arm (just about the only advantage of an automatic transmission is that you can pet your dog even at stoplights.)

That was when I found the other lump, on the side of his neck, hidden beneath the wealth of luxurious golden mane he had gotten from both of his show-ring champion parents. Giving up on trying to stay calm, I made it to the vet's somehow and stood, cold and worried, while Dr. Spindel gently and thoroughly examined Arthur.

Arthur, of course, had always loved his regular vet's quiet, focused attention, and this specialist vet was similarly attentive and genuinely affectionate to my eighty-pound puppy. Arthur truly enjoyed this examination as he did any human interaction, including vaccinations.

Then Dr. Spindel leaned down and kissed Arthur on top of his silken head.

That braced me for the terrible diagnosis: the cancer had come back yet again, and this time it was inoperable. I had not thought to peer at the roof of Arthur's mouth, but when the vet showed me, even I could see it was bad. The new tumor involved his entire upper jaw, from eyes to nose.

How had he been catching the frisbee with that mess in his mouth? It's a tribute to his heritage of hunting companions who waited patiently in a boat to dive into ice-crusted water to bring back a duck, working without complaint through personal and environmental conditions that would sideline a football player.

I declined the offer of radiation and chemotherapy for my furry chum; I did not want my beloved Arthur to go through that, just for a selfish chance to have him with me for a little longer. We were sent home with painkillers and Dr. Spindel's recommendation to love on him, keep him happy, and feed him anything he wanted.

We had always enjoyed long walks, but now every night we stayed out until dark. His energy remained inexhaustible, and his attitude exuberant as always. I pretended nothing was wrong, except for the pills I gave him, and his meals now shamelessly laden with the previously carefully rationed "people food."

But I watched both tumors grow, and after a month or so, started hearing him make a sort of snoring sound at night, as the one in his nose started to interfere with his breathing.

Then, on one of our walks, I had to stop and wait for him. He was still delighted to go, but it was physically simply too much no matter what his huge heart wanted, and walks were no longer practical.

I switched to just tossing the frisbee more or less toward him in the yard, and he loved it. At night he slept by my side on a blanket on the floor, his snoring getting louder. He started twitching in his sleep, but easily came out of it, waking instantly at my voice or touch.

Then one Sunday he made only a halfhearted effort at catching his beloved fabric frisbee, then sat panting, even though the day was cool. Just the day before he had leaped with all four feet in the air to catch the thing. Well, maybe he was having a bad day. We all do.

Monday he was worse, and Monday night it was clear he was uncomfortable despite the pain medication. He refused deli ham by hand.

I was faced with the most terrible decision a caretaker has to make: could I justify keeping him alive despite knowing he was no longer enjoying even little things, to put off saying goodbye? Sometimes, if you phrase a question honestly, the answer is obvious.

At the vet's, I sat on the floor with Arthur across my lap, and Dr. Spindel sat beside us. Even this experienced vet had tears. My beautiful companion had quickly become a favorite there, with his cheerful demeanor, habitual good manners, and indomitable spirit.

But now he was tired, and I'm grateful I could at least grant him a dignified passing -- a privilege denied our human loved ones. With self-discipline born of love, I clung to a veneer of calm and praised him softly while he slowly went to sleep in my arms. Afterwards I could (and did) indulge in a meltdown; but these last few moments were about Arthur's needs, not mine.

His ashes are in a box on the bookshelf, with a view of the door. Every night when I came home, he would wedge his nose in the crack of the door as I tried to open it, and every night I had to tell him to step back or have his nose squished.

I've left most of his toys scattered across the floor, but his fuzzy football I picked up, to put on the bookshelf next to him.

Thank you, to everyone who loved Arthur, many without ever meeting him. These snippets of his life put into words grant him a sort of immortality, so that even after I'm gone, people will read about him and love him.

About the Author

Calligrapher, illustrator, licensed falconer and wildlife rehabilitator, Donna Fritz lives on a small lake in a cozy cottage with two USDA and state licensed Opossums, two birds, one five-foot kingsnake, and Runi, a border collie mix from the Cayuga Dog Rescue, whose quiet love and support lent her the strength to finish this book.

Printed in the United States
By Bookmasters